SAVANNAH'S Afterlife

true tales of a
paranormal investigator

RYAN DUNN

4880 Lower Valley Road • Atglen, PA 19310

Cover concept by John Olenyik
Photography by Ryan Reese and Ryan Dunn
Designed by Brenda McCallum
Type set in Dead Secretary/Porcelain/Birch/Times

ISBN: 978-0-7643-4769-6
Printed in The United States of America

Schiffer Books are available at special discounts for bulk purchases for sales promotions or premiums. Special editions, including personalized covers, corporate imprints, and excerpts can be created in large quantities for special needs. For more information contact the publisher:

Published by Schiffer Publishing, Ltd.
4880 Lower Valley Road
Atglen, PA 19310
Phone: (610) 593-1777; Fax: (610) 593-2002
E-mail: Info@schifferbooks.com

For the largest selection of fine reference books on this and related subjects, please visit our website at **www.schifferbooks.com.** We are always looking for people to write books on new and related subjects. If you have an idea for a book, please contact us at proposals@schifferbooks.com.

This book may be purchased from the publisher. Please try your bookstore first. You may write for a free catalog.

DEDICATION

*I would first and foremost like to dedicate this book
to the Lord Jesus Christ my Savior for all of the blessings
bestowed upon me and my family over the years.
Without him nothing would be possible.*

I would like to also dedicate this book to my beautiful wife, Kim, for all of her love and continued support as I wrote this book. Thank you for being the most amazing woman on this planet! Paranormal research isn't always an easy life; thank you for being so understanding, even when our work has literally come home with us on more than one occasion.

Additionally, this book is for my two beautiful daughters, Jennifer and Addison. Thank you for always bringing a smile to my face.

For my father: God rest your soul, and may you find peace on the other side. If you ever decide to make contact, my ears are open.

For my mother: who somehow managed to raise us right, even though my brother and I were two of the wildest children ever.

For David, my brother: thank you for your support over the years.

For my father-in-law, David Dahlin, and my brother-in-law, Brandon Dahlin: thank you for being a part of this from the beginning.

For my mother-in-law, Jeanette: thank you for being there whenever I needed you.

For my sister-in-law, Sara Dahlin: thank you for being so awesome!

And finally, for my grandfather, Bill Dunn: I have always looked up to you, thank you for being such a great role model.

CONTENTS

ACKNOWLEDGMENTS

This book was written only after years of thorough research and multiple investigations, and I have a lot of people to thank for their help along the way. Many business owners have allowed us full access to their locations for overnight investigations, and many others have assisted our team in many other ways. This could get quite lengthy and, if so, I do apologize, but I feel that I should give credit where credit is due.

Thank you to my dear friend and graphic designer Alan Gallardo for all of your amazing work. Thank you to Ryan Reese for all of your hard work with the 3-D Ghost Hunters and for your amazing photography in this book. Thank you to Guieneverre Cutlip for all of your hard work with the 3-D Ghost Hunters and for editing this book before I sent off the final manuscript. Thank you to Brandon, Sara, and David Dahlin for your hard work with the 3-D Ghost Hunters over the years.

Everyone at the Georgia Historical Society on Gaston Street has been more than helpful in assisting me with all of my historical research: thank you for being so patient with me! I owe a huge thanks to Phillip and Charlene Brannan, the owners of the Boar's Head Restaurant on River Street, for allowing us full access to their building to conduct our research. Also, thank you to Rose Gillespie, who works there as well, for sending all of your guests on our tour. I would like to thank Rocky, Jane, and Sarah Reed for allowing us to investigate the Amethyst Inn and for all of your continued support over the years. Thank you to Billy Kitchens and Rob Britton at the Chart House Restaurant for one of the most memorable investigations ever.

A huge debt of gratitude is owed to the Bradley family for allowing us to investigate their family business. Thank you to Brandi Cockram and Gene Beeco of the Moon River Brewing Company, and to Regina Graham at the River Street Inn. Also, thank you to Patrick Godley and his family, and to Cody White and his mother, Tammy, for such a great investigation at the 17hundred90 Inn. Many thanks to the Meece family that owns the Savannah Theatre and to Dru Jones, the theatre manager, who has the best one-liners of anyone I know. Thank you to Daniel Brown at Fort McAllister for allowing us to investigate, even though you are a skeptic! Thank you to Tyler Duddy and Grant Rogers at the Foley House for not only the investigation, but for all of the guests you continue to send on our tours. Thank you to Francis Sein and Liz Kem at the Savannah Harley Davidson on River Street.

Thank you to Deborah and her team at Past Life Investigations of Georgia for your support and for taking so many cases when our workload was too much—you guys rock! Thank you to Frank Sulkowski, Julie Eisenman, and Biff Flowers at WJCL ABC News and WTGS FOX News 28 here in Savannah for all of the filming and the support. Thank you to Adam Van Brimmer, Jeremiah Johnson, and Kenneth Rosen for your articles on us in the *Savannah Morning News*.

I think this pretty much covers it, and if there is anyone else that I did forget to mention, I deeply apologize, and appreciate your understanding and assistance.

—*Ryan Dunn*

INTRODUCTION

The age old question still exists: Are ghosts real? For thousands of years, tales of the paranormal have circulated throughout most societies. If you research the world's various religions, you can find evidence of the spirit world in most of the holy books. With all of the innovative technology readily available to us today, we are finally able to capture compelling evidence to prove that ghosts do indeed exist. Through the use of audio and video recorders, temperature gauges and EMF detectors, as well as other scientific equipment, modern-day investigators are able to capture evidence of the paranormal that will sway the mind of even the most determined skeptic.

Before I get too far, please permit me to introduce myself. My name is Ryan Dunn, and I am a paranormal investigator in Savannah, Georgia, known to many as America's most haunted city. In 2010, I founded the *3-D Ghost Hunters*, a paranormal investigation research team, with my brother-in-law, Brandon Dahlin, and my father-in-law, David Dahlin. The name itself originated from all three of our last initials. My wife, Kim, also joined the team, as did my sister-in-law, Sara Dahlin. Since founding our team, we have had the opportunity to investigate some of the most haunted locations throughout the city. We have been in these places for hours on end and we have experienced the paranormal activity in these locations firsthand. From seeing apparitions manifest themselves, to being physically pushed and scratched by unseen forces, we have seen it all. The group has evolved over the years, and now consists of my wife Kim, Ryan Reese, our photographer and equipment tech, and me. We are now known as the *Savannah Ghost Research Society*, and we still conduct paranormal investigations throughout our historic city on a regular basis.

It all began in April of 2010, when Kim and I decided to move our family to Savannah, Georgia. We had previously come to Savannah on our honeymoon a few years earlier, and we fell in love with the place almost immediately. We vowed to eventually move to the city, and three years later we packed everything we owned and left North Carolina to begin a new chapter in our lives. We wanted to start our own catering business and Savannah seemed the perfect market for it. With Savannah being one of the biggest wedding destination cities in the United States, we knew the business would flourish there. When we moved here, our two daughters were only two and four years old, so it seemed like the perfect time. We selected a beautiful Victorian row house in the famed Historic District as our new home. If we were going to live in Savannah, we were determined to live downtown. Our home was only two blocks from Forsyth Park, which was perfect for our girls. The house was built in the early 1890s and, little did we know at the time, that the place itself was haunted.

My wife and I have always been intrigued by the paranormal, but we had never made the decision to begin seriously researching the subject until we moved to Savannah. We began our research by setting up an investigation at Colonial Park Cemetery only two weeks after we moved to the city. We could barely call this an investigation because, at the time, we were just amateur ghost hunters looking for a good scare. It wasn't until about six months later that we began conducting serious scientific and historical research into the paranormal. That particular evening we were armed with only a digital audio voice recorder, an EMF detector, and a flashlight. The results of that night's investigation, however, were nonetheless astounding. We returned from the cemetery that evening with real voice recordings of the dead on our audio recorders, and they were direct responses to the questions that we were asking! When we realized that we could not only communicate with the dead, but also document the activity, we began to investigate the paranormal as much as time would allow. In the beginning, we were very amateurish at our work, but it didn't take long for the newfound hobby to turn into a professional business.

I first began my research by studying those who came before me: parapsychologists and researchers who were highly accredited for their work. Instead of copying what everyone was doing on all of the ghost shows on television, I wanted to know what the real researchers were discovering. I wanted to study the researchers in the field and read their case files. I spent years studying the works of Rosemary Ellen Guiley, Loyd Auerbach, Troy Taylor, Hans Holzer, Ed and Lorraine Warren, John Zaffis, and many others. I founded the 3-D Ghost Hunters here in Savannah with my in-laws and my wife Kim, and we began to investigate many of the most haunted locations in the city. We tried various pieces of equipment in the beginning and, through trial and error, we quickly learned what worked best for our team. Although Kim and I are the only original members left, we still continue where the 3-D Ghost Hunters left off with our new team, the Savannah Ghost Research Society.

We only use audio and video recording equipment, temperature gauges, EMF and motion detectors, and a few other pieces of equipment to conduct our research. We do not use Ouija boards, dowsing rods, or anything of that nature. We do believe that they can work, but we attempt to document everything from a more scientific point of view. Our main priority is to ensure that all of the information gathered while conducting a paranormal investigation is as accurate as possible. We use only scientific methods and equipment to obtain our data, and we try to find a reasonable and rational explanation for whatever occurs. A paranormal explanation is always our last conclusion.

We also work with the Georgia Historical Society in Savannah, prior to all of our investigations, in order to get a detailed, exhaustive, year-by-year history of every location. Only by doing this are we able to find out what really happened at any given location to explain the paranormal activity that occurs there.

Not long after forming the 3-D Ghost Hunters, we began to receive numerous calls concerning paranormal activity. Calls were coming in left and right from haunted restaurants, inns, and private residences, as well as many other places around town. About a year and a half after we founded our team, I was contacted by Frank Sulkowski, the assistant news director and head sports director for WJCL *ABC News* and WTGS *FOX News 28* in Savannah. The news station wanted to do a story about ghosts in Savannah, and Frank asked me if he could attend an investigation with us for the story. We invited him along on an investigation of the historic Savannah Theatre, and the evidence we captured that evening was so compelling that they eventually gave us our own television series entitled *Spooky Town*.

In the summer of 2012, I was approached by A&E Biography's hit television show *My Ghost Story: Caught on Camera*. They wanted to know if I had any cases with some great hard evidence for the show. I emailed them the case file and evidence from the Savannah Theatre investigation, and they invited me and Dru Jones, the theatre's stage manager, out to Los Angeles to film on their set. The show aired in December of 2012, and my wife and I started to realize that, although we had moved to Savannah to open a catering business, we were being pulled in a completely different direction.

We opened our walking ghost tour company, Afterlife Tours, in April of 2013, and began doing paranormal research as a full-time job. Our tour company is a bit more unique than other ghost tours, as we have fully investigated every stop on our tour. We play real paranormal evidence at every stop captured by our research team as well. It adds another level to the traditional ghost tour when you can hear real voices of the dead and you can see real apparitions on video. In addition, we debunk urban folklore and give the real reasons why the places are haunted. If you happen to be in town, we would love to have you come out and experience the tour firsthand to hear these recordings and watch the videos that we have captured at each location.

Our paranormal research team, the Savannah Ghost Research Society, remains a nonprofit organization. We do not charge for any of our investigations, and we are completely funded by donations and fundraisers. We still continue to investigate Savannah's most haunted locations on a regular basis, and we remain very active in the city's paranormal community.

Before you begin reading, I did want to briefly mention some common paranormal terminology used throughout this book. You will see the term Electronic Voice Phenomena (EVP) mentioned in many chapters. An EVP is an audio recording of a spirit's voice. These can be captured on any type of audio recording device, whether it be a micro cassette recorder or digital voice recorder, and they are one of the most compelling pieces of paranormal evidence. The way it works is simple. You go into a haunted location with an audio recording device and begin asking questions to elicit a response. In most cases, you will not hear anything while you are there, but, on the playback, you can often hear unexplainable direct voice responses to your questions.

Many ghost enthusiasts like to make it seem that these entities are somehow getting into your recorder and magically putting their voice into the recording, which is kind of a hard pill to swallow. My theory, however, is much simpler and seems to make much more sense. I believe that it works a lot like a dog whistle. Most human beings cannot hear a dog whistle, although we do know that the sound exists. It works the same way with spirit voices. They are answering our questions while we are right there; it's just that we human beings cannot hear on that particular frequency level. The microchip in any audio recorder—even the cheapest one you may find—picks up on a wider frequency range than the human ear. That is why you do not hear the voices of the dead until you play back the recording. When you play it back, the recorder itself has imprinted the spirit voice into a sound discernible to human ears.

This is also the reason that we film with full-spectrum lights on our video cameras. These lights cover the full spectrum of light, including UV and infrared, which cannot be seen with the naked human eye. This could also possibly explain why dogs and cats are more sensitive to the paranormal, since they can hear and see on a much wider frequency and range.

This book compiles nearly four years of in-depth paranormal and historical research in and around the city of Savannah. All of the stories and histories here are 100 percent fact, having been fully researched. Real names and locations have been used throughout. The only time you will find that names have been omitted is in the private residences chapter, but even then some of the real names have been used. All of the events that you will read about are real. There has been no stretching of the truth or taking liberty with events due to timing or any other reason. Every chapter involves the story of some of the most haunted locations in Savannah, as well as the investigation of the place itself. This book is as real as it gets.

Thank you and happy hunting,
Ryan Dunn

CHAPTER 1

SAVANNAH'S TRAGIC PAST

Before we delve into the paranormal side of Savannah, it is important to understand a little bit about the dark past that surrounds this charming city. In the 1990s, Duke University's Parapsychology Department nicknamed the city of Savannah "America's Most Haunted City," and with good reason. In its mere 280-year history, Savannah has befallen more than its share of tragic events. From wars, fires, diseases, and floods, Savannah has witnessed devastation in almost every form. In addition to all of the deaths from these events, slavery caused a great deal of death and suffering in the city for many years. The slaves brought with them their beliefs in Voodoo and root work, which is still very present in Savannah and the surrounding areas to this day.

The city of Savannah itself was established by an English General named James Edward Oglethorpe. England was dealing with a huge problem of overcrowding in prisons. When you went into debt in England, you were thrown into a debtor's prison until you could pay off your debt. Not only were you unable to work to raise the necessary money while you were incarcerated, but they also charged you room and board. One of Oglethorpe's friends died of Lupus in one of these prisons because he went into debt after a book he wrote on architecture didn't do so well. Oglethorpe himself felt compelled to come up with a solution to alleviate the problem, so he approached King George II with an idea. Oglethorpe suggested that England establish a colony in the New World in order to better help England deal with their poor. Also, building this colony would establish a new trade route, and act as a buffer between the colonies of North Carolina and Florida.

On November 17, 1732, General Oglethorpe, along with 114 colonists, departed from Gravesend, England, on a ship named the *Anne*. They landed a few months later on the banks of the Savannah River, on February 12, 1733. Georgia, the 13th colony, was named after King George II himself, and Savannah became its very first city. In the first few years of this new colony of Savannah, strong spirits, lawyers, and slavery were banned. Wine and ale was legal, however, and the ban on slavery was later repealed in the year 1750.

Towards the end of the 1700s, Savannah was hit hard by the British forces during the American Revolution. Only a few days after Christmas, on December 29, 1778, over 3,000 British forces arrived in Savannah. Defended by only 850 soldiers, our poor city was captured in no time. We lost 83 soldiers that day, whereas the British went away mostly unscathed with only 7 casualties. After this battle, British troops quickly began to occupy the city. It wasn't until nearly a year later that residents decided to try to take their city back.

On October 9, 1779, one of the bloodiest battles of the American Revolution took place in what is now part of Savannah's Historic District. American colonists teamed up with French forces to capture the British Fort, the Spring Hill Redoubt. The troops led a surprise attack just before dawn on the fort. As the battle raged on, the trenches surrounding the fort quickly began to fill with bodies. A truce was called less than an hour into the battle in order for the colonists and the French to bury their dead. Although the British had only lost 120 men, the colonist's death toll was over 800 soldiers. In order to avoid the spread of disease, the majority of those soldiers were buried in a mass grave near where they fell.

Savannah also suffered greatly from multiple fires that destroyed over half of the city. The first of these fires occurred in November of 1796 in a bake shop near the old city market. In only a matter of hours, 229 buildings were destroyed throughout the city. One of the biggest fires to devastate Savannah, however, occurred on January 11, 1820, at around 2 o'clock in the morning. This fire began at a livery stable near the old city market, close to what is now Ellis Square. Within the next few hours, 463 buildings were completely destroyed.

Although these fires destroyed much of the city, it was the numerous Yellow Fever epidemics that really took a toll on Savannah's early citizens. The first Yellow Fever epidemic to ravage Savannah began in 1820 when 666 citizens were lost to the fever. Although this disease was transferred by mosquitoes, early citizens of the city were convinced that the epidemic was communicable, and it wasn't until many years later that the true cause of the disease was discovered. In 1854, Yellow Fever once again returned to the city, this time causing a death toll of 1,040.

As if this weren't enough, Savannah suffered a great hurricane that resulted in a large flood that same year. In 1876, Savannah experienced its last and most devastating epidemic of Yellow Fever. According to Evelyn Ward Gay, in her book *The Medical Profession in Georgia 1733-1983*: "In 1876 there were 1,594 deaths from a population of 20,561 in a period of five months, or one in 13."

In December of 1864, Union General William Tecumseh Sherman ended his March to Sea in Savannah. When he arrived, city officials met Sherman at the city gates and surrendered the city to him. Although there were no battles fought within the city of Savannah itself, both Fort Pulaski and Fort McAllister (on the outside of town) did see action during the War Between the States. Due to being severely outnumbered, both forts were easily defeated by Sherman and his troops.

It seems that as soon as Savannah would overcome one tragic event, another would befall the city shortly after. For many years, the city itself was said to be cursed, but somehow its citizens still managed to prevail. These events could easily be the cause of the paranormal activity that surrounds the city of Savannah. With all of its grim past, it is no wonder that Savannah remains to this day to be one of the most haunted cities in the United States.

CHAPTER 2
The Old Brick Graveyard
THE COLONIAL PARK CEMETERY
INVESTIGATION

The broken headstones lining the east wall once marked graves in this cemetery.
It is no longer known where they were originally placed. *Photo by Ryan Dunn*

THE HISTORY

In the heart of Savannah's famed Historic District, you will find the Colonial Park Cemetery, the second oldest Christian burial ground in the city, and the oldest still intact. The colony's original cemetery, which is the only one that is older, remains under the buildings south of Wright Square. Opened to colonists in the year 1750, the Colonial Park Cemetery accepted burials until 1853, when it was closed due to overcrowding. Many of Savannah's founding families are buried throughout the cemetery, as well as numerous revolutionary war heroes, duelists, and many of Savannah's early colonists. Most notably, the cemetery is home to Button Gwinnett, one of the signers of the Declaration of Independence. In addition, there are numerous unmarked graves throughout the cemetery.

Also known as "The Old Burying Ground" and "The Old Brick Graveyard," the cemetery contains nearly 600 headstones, yet historians and archaeologists have determined that there are approximately 10,000 graves altogether. This cemetery used to be much larger than it is now. Presumably, the City pulled up tombstones in order to make way for both a city street and sidewalk on Abercorn Street, next to the burial ground, in 1896. As with most other hidden cemeteries in town, the headstones were moved, yet the bodies remained. In this same year, the City of Savannah took on a renovation project to clean up the old cemetery. It was in such disrepair that many broken headstones were scattered throughout the grounds. Not knowing where they belonged after so many years, the Park and Tree Commission mounted the headstones along the east wall of the cemetery, where they still remain to this day.

In 1820, an unyielding Yellow Fever epidemic ravaged the city of Savannah. During its toll, the city tragically lost one tenth of its population. Many of these Yellow Fever victims were interred at Colonial Park Cemetery. A historical marker in the cemetery honors the Yellow Fever Victims of 1820. On the marker it says that nearly 700 victims died of the disease in that year and are buried in Colonial Park Cemetery. The marker was placed here in 1970 by the Trustees Garden Club. The reason they didn't put the exact number of victims on the marker, but merely rounded the number up to 700 was for good reason. There were actually 666 people to die of Yellow Fever in the year 1820, and they didn't want to place this evil number on the marker—they rounded the death toll up to "nearly 700" just to be safe.

There are a lot of stories that derive from misreading this marker and say that there is a mass grave beneath it where nearly 700 victims are buried. Although it makes for a great story, this is untrue. There are nearly 700 Yellow Fever victims buried here, but they are scattered throughout the whole cemetery and not in one large, mass grave.

There were numerous reports of people being buried alive in Colonial Park, especially during the height of the 1820 Yellow Fever Epidemic. The disease could lead to paralysis, and oftentimes people were pronounced dead when in fact they were still alive. This, unfortunately, often led to premature burials. In an effort to prevent a misdiagnosis, corpses were allegedly buried with a string tied around their finger, which led out of the casket and above ground. The other end of the string was attached to a bell hanging from a stick that was posted near the headstone of the grave. Community citizens took turns performing "graveyard shift" in order to listen for bells ringing throughout

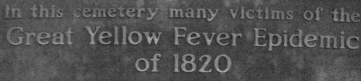

In this cemetery many victims of the
Great Yellow Fever Epidemic
of 1820
were buried.

Nearly 700 Savannahians died
that year, including two local
physicians who lost their lives
caring for the stricken.

Several epidemics followed. In 1854
The Savannah Benevolent Association
was organized to aid the families
of the fever victims.

THE TRUSTEES GARDEN CLUB 1970

This historical marker honors the many Yellow Fever victims buried here in 1820. The exact death toll in that year from the fever totaled 666. *Photo by Ryan Reese* the night. If a bell started ringing, the unfortunate person on duty that evening would have the dreadful task of rushing to save the victim from suffocation. This is supposedly where the phrases "graveyard shift," "dead ringer," and "saved by the bell" originated.

Although I did not find any proof of the "coffin bells" in this particular cemetery, I did find proof that similar devices were patented in the United States in order to reduce the number of premature burials. These contraptions were attached to what were known as "safety coffins," and some were equipped with elaborate bell and cord systems.

For many years, the fear of being buried alive has frightened people the world over. Frederic Chopin's last words from his deathbed were: "Swear to make them cut me open, so that I won't be buried alive," and President George Washington said: "Have me decently buried, but do not let my body be put into a vault in less than two days after I am dead." It seems that the fear of being buried alive was prevalent in those times, as well as here in Savannah.

The origins of the phrases "graveyard shift," "dead ringer," and "saved by the bell," however, had nothing to do with being buried alive. Although they do tie together a great ghost story, they come from much less disturbing backgrounds. The term "saved by the bell" was first used in the late 1800s to describe a boxing match. Someone was "saved by the bell" if they could survive a round of clobbering without being knocked out. The phrase "dead ringer" has nothing to do with the ringing of bells. It actually means "exact replica," and was coined from horse racing at the end of the 19th century. And, finally, the phrase "graveyard shift," also originated around the same time as the other two. This term has nothing to do with premature interment, but referred to working the late shift from 12 a.m. to 8 a.m., when everything was dark and desolate.

Another popular myth surrounding the Colonial Park Cemetery is that the city's old dueling grounds were near its south end. This is probably not true. Dueling was illegal in Savannah, although it still did occur. It did not occur, however, in Colonial Park Cemetery. Duelists would take a very short boat trip across the river to Hutchinson Island, South Carolina. There they could duel without the fear of being arrested for murder. In most cases, the loser of the duel was still brought back across the river and usually interred at Colonial Park Cemetery. There is a plaque in the cemetery dedicated to the many lives lost because of dueling over the early years of the colony that states that many duelists are still buried there.

Quite possibly the most famous ghost story concerning Colonial Park is the horrific story of a man named Rene Rondolier Asche. According to legend, Rene was born to a French family in Savannah during the early 1800s. He was a massive sixteen pounds at birth, and he was born with a disfigured face. By the time Rene was sixteen years old, he was over seven feet tall. Due to his size, he had abnormal strength, and would accidentally kill small animals with his heavy touch. It was also said that he would enter secret tunnels under the cemetery and play with the dead carcasses of these animals. One morning, the body of a young girl was found near the dreaded Foley's Alley section of town and Rene was blamed for the murder. The townspeople dragged him from his home and he was supposedly lynched in the southwest corner of Warren Square. Rene is reported to haunt Colonial Park Cemetery, looking for his animals, or perhaps another victim.

To begin with, there is no record of Rene Rondolier Asche ever existing in Savannah, and the murder of the young girl never took place. The story is complete urban legend, yet it still circulates throughout Savannah quite a bit. This story gained much unneeded notoriety when it was featured on ABC Family's *Scariest Places on Earth*, hosted by Linda Blair. The show depicted the grave of a little girl murdered by Rene, yet the grave they identified was that of Little Gracie Watson, who was not even buried at Colonial Park Cemetery, but ten miles away at Bonaventure Cemetery—and she died in 1890 at six years of age of pneumonia! Although there are a lot of myths surrounding Colonial Park Cemetery, there are much better ghost stories here that are actually true.

During the Civil War, Union General William Tecumseh Sherman led his famous "March to the Sea" that ended in Savannah in December of 1864. Shortly after he arrived, he presented the city of Savannah to President Abraham Lincoln as a Christmas present in a famous telegraph. During the Union Army's occupation of Savannah, many of Sherman's troops camped out in the old cemetery. Due to the cold weather in December, many of his troops broke into the family crypts for shelter to stay warm, as well as to pillage and loot them. These crypts had stairs that went down about five to six feet underground, and they were equipped with three to five slabs on either side of the walls, where the corpses would be placed. The corpses were merely wrapped in a shroud, instead of being placed in a casket, for a quick decomposition. This was done for good reason, because once the family crypt filled up and someone new passed away, a new crypt wasn't constructed—Savannahians just became more creative.

When all of the slabs were filled up and a new family member passed away, the oldest skeleton would be disassembled and placed into a box at the base of the crypt. The newest corpse would then take its place on the slab. These boxes were known as "bone boxes" and, over time, they contained the remains of multiple family members. Crypts were also fashioned to resemble large beds, in order to represent an eternal resting place, with the front and back appearing to be the headboard and the footboard. All of these "beds" also face the east, since that is where the sun rises. The feet of the corpses were pointed east and the heads pointed west. According to Christian religion, Jesus Christ will return from the east. When he calls his people home, they will be facing their maker when they rise from their graves.

Aside from desecrating the family crypts, Sherman's troops have also been blamed for the defacing of many headstones throughout Colonial Park Cemetery. For instance, you may find a headstone of a male who died at three years of age, but left behind a twenty-nine-year-old daughter. Some peoples' ages are in the thousands at the age of death, and other ridiculous, impossible inscriptions are seen throughout the cemetery's many headstones. The changing of the headstones is attributed to a cruel prank performed by General Sherman's soldiers. However, the cemetery was also used as a camping area for British troops occupying Savannah during the American Revolution. There is a possibility that it could have been their doing, or possibly just the result of some bored teenagers long ago. The damage was done so many years ago that we do not now know who caused the vandalism. Although we are not sure who originally changed the headstones, most Savannahians still like to blame General Sherman and his troops.

19

Colonial Park Cemetery, the oldest intact Christian burial ground in
Savannah's Historic District. *Photo by Ryan Reese*

These family crypts were purposely fashioned to resemble large beds to signify eternal rest. *Photo by Ryan Reese*

On November 16, 1901, a strange incident occurred at Colonial Park Cemetery that remains unsolved to this day. A man named Samuel T. Baker was leaving work late one evening from the accounting firm of John Lynes and Company. He would always cut through the cemetery on his way home from work every night to save time. On this particular evening, he stopped by Gayou's Barbershop on Broughton Street for a quick shave. On his way out of the shop, he purchased a bottle of whiskey to take to a sick friend on the way home. In those days, whiskey was a common remedy for colds and other ailments, especially in the good old city of Savannah. As he walked out of the door and continued south towards the cemetery, he placed the bottle of whiskey inside his breast coat pocket for safekeeping and continued on his way. Although he was only about eight minutes away from his house, Samuel T. Baker never made it home that evening.

Three teenage boys later discovered an elderly man that night in the cemetery lying on the ground. The man was moaning and bleeding from the head, and he smelled strongly of liquor. The three boys went around the corner to the police barracks on Oglethorpe Avenue, which borders the old cemetery on the east, and explained to the officer on duty what they had just witnessed. The officer headed over to the cemetery to investigate for himself. As he arrived on the scene, he discovered Samuel T. Baker lying on the ground, muttering unintelligible words. He was indeed bleeding from the head and he smelled strongly of alcohol. A broken whiskey bottle was found on the ground near the man, so the officer determined him to be drunk and promptly arrested him for public intoxication. Later that evening, Baker's son-in-law, E.M. Hopkins, arrived at the police station to report the man missing. The officer on duty then explained to Hopkins that he had just arrested Mr. Baker a few hours earlier for public drunkenness. After telling the whole story to Hopkins, the officer released Samuel T. Baker to his son-in-law who took him home, where he later died at around 6:30 that morning, at the age of 62.

Samuel T. Baker had died from massive injury and trauma to the head. He had been severely beaten that evening, shortly before the three teenage boys had found him. Also, he was not intoxicated, but the bottle of whiskey in his coat pocket had been broken during his altercation, which explained why he strongly reeked of alcohol. The reason he had been muttering unintelligible words was not due to drunkenness, but because he was suffering from massive concussions at the time. One of the most puzzling things about the whole case, however, is the fact that Mr. Baker still had money on him after he was accosted, which meant that he was not robbed. No one could find a motive as to why someone would want to murder an innocent old man.

Many years later, in 2005, a SCAD (Savannah College of Art and Design) student was in the cemetery one sunny afternoon sitting on a bench reading a book when she happened to look up and witness a man stumbling towards her. He was wearing a long, gray coat and appeared to be bleeding from the head as he staggered her way. As he got closer, she screamed as loud as she possibly could, and the man suddenly disappeared. Could this have been the ghost of Samuel T. Baker still haunting the old cemetery? It is quite possible, and to this day his murder remains unsolved.

The front entrance of Colonial Park Cemetery erected by the Daughters of the
American Revolution in 1913. *Photo by Ryan Dunn*

THE INVESTIGATION

With all of the paranormal activity in Colonial Park Cemetery, this location became the site of our very first investigation as the 3-D Ghost Hunters in April of 2010. The investigation began in the wee hours of the morning at around 3 a.m. I was accompanied by Kim, and Brandon and Sara Dahlin. As we arrived at the cemetery, the wind was blowing fiercely and there was a full moon in the sky. These weather conditions only added to the overall feeling of not being alone. We began our investigation by sitting on a bench and asking questions, in hopes of capturing some EVPs. Although we felt like a ghostly presence was with us throughout the investigation, we didn't hear or see anything that we could not explain with our own eyes and ears while on location. When we arrived back home and started reviewing the evidence, however, we found shocking discoveries.

During the beginning of the investigation, Sara became frightened and said: "I can't do this, I'm going to leave." A female spirit then angrily growled "Leave" into the audio recorder. At this discovery we all realized that Colonial Park Cemetery was definitely as haunted as it was rumored to be, but this was only the beginning.

Later on, during the investigation, I asked: "Who are we talking to?" The audio recorder captured the voice of a small female child who simply answered "Kate." Not realizing that the entity had responded to our question (because most EVPs are only heard on the playback), I asked again about ten seconds later, "Who are we talking to?" The same small voice then replied: "The dead." Later in the evening I asked: "Are you a good spirit or a bad spirit?" A male entity suddenly replied: "Good spirit." To hear these voices on recording and find no logical explanation for them was unreal. They were clear responses to our questions, and no one, save us, was around in the old cemetery for hundreds of yards.

As we prepared to leave the investigation, we managed to capture one more haunting audio clip. We were packing up and getting ready to head out of the cemetery when our audio recorder captured the voice of a small girl whispering: "Come back, come here." Perhaps after many years of loneliness, the spirits were finally glad to have someone acknowledging them.

In any case, whether you are just strolling through during the day or passing by at night, be aware that you are not alone when you are near Colonial Park Cemetery, the oldest cemetery still intact in the City of Savannah.

CHAPTER 3

No Rest at 12 West
THE 12 WEST OGLETHORPE
INVESTIGATION

Many people have some story of a haunted house in their hometown—one that causes people to cross the street when passing by, small children to scurry past hurriedly, and locals to spin yarns about its tragic history. Here in Savannah, however, we literally have hundreds. If you could narrow down the hundreds of haunted buildings in Savannah into just one to fit that same description, then the house located at 12 West Oglethorpe Avenue would be that house. This property has enthralled ghost hunters and paranormal enthusiasts alike for many years. The psychic energy alone radiating from the house is so immense that the property has remained vacant since 1985. Although it is prime real estate located on beautiful Oglethorpe Avenue, which is one of the busiest streets in the Historic District, no one seems to want to take on the challenge of dealing with the paranormal activity that surrounds the place.

DR. BROWN

One of the most popular stories related to this particular house concerns a man by the name of Dr. Brown. During the height of Savannah's last Yellow Fever Epidemic of 1876, a man named Dr. Brown decided to move his wife and two children to the cursed city to try and find a cure. With the death toll rising rapidly, both his wife and children begged him not to move them there. "Everyone in Savannah is dying," they told him. "We are going to catch the Fever and die." Optimistic about finding a cure for the Fever, however, the doctor moved his family to Savannah against their wishes.

Dr. Brown set up his office in the downstairs parlor of his family's residence at 12 West Oglethorpe Avenue, and victims riddled with the disease would arrive at his front steps, knocking on the door three times to signify that they were Yellow Fever victims in need of treatment. He experimented on several patients in the home while trying to find a cure for the disease, but to no avail. One by one, his wife and two children contracted the disease and died. Over time, the burden of the death of his family became too much for him. The doctor bricked himself up in the top left bedroom of the home to kill himself. He supposedly haunts the halls of this home searching for the souls of his departed family.

Rumor has it, if you knock on the front door three times, the doctor will come and answer the door.

This is a great ghost story, but the house at 12 West Oglethorpe was built in 1898, and the last Yellow Fever Epidemic occurred in 1876. Not only do the years not match up, but there is no record of anyone by the last name of Brown ever living in, or working in, that home. There was a prior structure located at 12 West Oglethorpe Avenue years before, but once again, no record of the name Brown.

12 West Oglethorpe Avenue, one of the most haunted houses in Savannah. *Photo by Ryan Reese*

The present structure was built for Beirne Gordon, who was partners with William Washington Gordon (founder of the Central of Georgia Railroad and father of Juliette Gordon Low). It was later owned by the Elk's Lodge from the 1930s until the 1980s, and then it became a Montessori school for young children. The school was known as the Savannah School of Performing Arts; and they accepted students from ages three to twelve years of age. The building then became abandoned in 1985 when the school moved out, and the home has remained vacant ever since.

THE JEWISH CEMETERY

Although the Dr. Brown story may not be true, the house is indeed haunted. The reason for the haunting of 12 West Oglethorpe, however, dates back much further than the 1800s.

In 1733, forty-two Jewish immigrants left from England by ship and arrived in Savannah about five months after the colony's first settlers, on July 11. Facing religious persecution in Europe, they were eager for a fresh start in the New World. Although Savannah already had a Christian burial ground in place, the Jewish community needed their own land to bury their dead. General James Edward Oglethorpe and the Trustees of the colony decided to allot a cemetery plot just outside of the city for a Jewish burial ground. As the city grew over the years, however, the land containing the Jewish Cemetery was needed for expansion. All of the headstones were moved to the new Jewish Cemetery just south of the city, but none of the corpses were moved. This was not out of sheer laziness, but out of the fear of spreading disease. Many of the early colonists had died of communicable diseases, so there was a natural fear of reintroducing these viruses back into the colony and creating an epidemic if the corpses were to be exhumed. It was also thought that Yellow Fever in those days was contracted by human-to-human

This monument marks the original Jewish cemetery, dating back to 1733. *Photo by Ryan Dunn*

contact. People infected with the disease were often quarantined because they had no idea at the time that the disease was actually transferred by mosquitoes. In addition, our early colonists were from England, where they had dealt with the Bubonic plague hundreds of years earlier. They were not about to take any chances by reinterring any corpses, so they left all of the bodies where they were and continued on with the expansion of the city.

This cemetery is now under the house located at 12 West Oglethorpe Avenue, as well as the First Presbyterian Church nearby, and under Oglethorpe Avenue itself. 12 West Oglethorpe does have a basement, so most of the corpses are no longer under this particular house, but it is over top of the original Jewish Cemetery of 1733. The only visible sign left of the old burial ground is a small monument in the median of Oglethorpe Avenue. Listed on the back of the monument are the names of sixteen people still interred in this cemetery. It goes on to say that there are doubtless many more interred here whose names are not now known. With all of these unmarked graves, there is no wonder as to why 12 West Oglethorpe is so haunted.

FIRE!

Although this house has been abandoned since 1985, a fire broke out in the home in 2009. In the spring of 2009, some teenagers were going around town lighting dumpsters on fire as an immature and dangerous prank. They decided to start a fire in one of the dumpsters located directly behind the old house. The back end of the house at 12 West Oglethorpe soon caught fire from the dumpster in the alley, and flames quickly engulfed the home.

I had the opportunity in 2010 to interview one of the firemen called out to the scene that night. It took the firefighters over three and a half hours to put the fire out, so, by city ordinance, the firemen were required to do what was called "fire watch." This meant that all of the men had to spend the night in the house, just in case the fire decided to reignite. This way they would be there with their hoses and equipment to prevent a historic building from burning to the ground. Out of sheer boredom, the men started telling ghost stories about the old house in order to pass the time. The firemen weren't aware of the real history surrounding the home, so it didn't take long for the Dr. Brown story to surface. As soon as it did, the men started daring each other to go to the upstairs bedroom where the old doctor had supposedly committed suicide many years before.

The first fireman slowly climbed the stairs and entered the bedroom. Suddenly, all of the men heard a blood-curdling scream from above, and the fireman came sprinting down the stairs. He looked at his fellow firemen and said: "I don't care what you guys say about me, but I am going to sleep in the truck. I have had enough of this house. You can say all that you want, but I'm outta here."

Throughout the rest of the evening, the other firemen poked fun at him for being scared of the house, but he still slept in the truck parked on Oglethorpe Avenue nonetheless. The man has never spoken about what happened to him in the upstairs bedroom that evening, and still, to this day, no one knows. Whatever it was, it definitely gave him a good scare. The other firemen who stayed in the house that night reported hearing strange sounds coming from upstairs throughout the evening, as well as experiencing uncomfortable feelings while in the home. They even heard footsteps climbing slowly down the stairs towards them, although they were the only ones in the house.

THE INVESTIGATION

In 2010, we were finally able to witness the haunting of 12 West Oglethorpe firsthand. To gain access to this house was the Holy Grail of ghost hunting in Savannah, and we were honored to finally get the chance to go inside. Once we arrived there for the investigation, our excitement quickly turned to fear. I would be lying if I said that we never get scared during these investigations, but that is also partly the reason we are in this business. The house itself had a very unsettling feeling as soon as we crossed the threshold into the entranceway. Although it had been more than a year since the fire, the house still smelled strongly of smoke. It smelled as if the fire was still smoldering, and another underlying noxious odor permeated the air. There was extensive fire and water damage throughout the house, so every step you took put you further at risk of getting hurt. We knew as soon as we had arrived that we had stumbled onto a paranormal goldmine, so right away we began unpacking our equipment and preparing for a long night of investigating.

Later in the evening, as I was walking down the hallway videotaping on the second floor, my camera suddenly powered down for no apparent reason. As I looked up, I saw a black shadow person cross the hallway right in front of me from one bedroom to the other. This black mass had a human shape and was three dimensional, but I could not make out any features. It couldn't have been more than five feet away, and it was almost seven feet tall! I froze for a second, and then followed it to the bedroom into which it had disappeared, only to find that there was nothing there. The room was completely empty. Whatever it was, it had suddenly vanished. Not only had it manifested itself, but it had also completely drained my camera, which was not operable for the rest of the investigation. This entity had decided to show itself to me, and I could find no logical explanation for what I had witnessed.

In addition to several personal experiences throughout the investigation, we captured multiple pieces of compelling audio evidence as well. One of the scariest EVPs was captured in the second floor hallway where I had encountered the shadow figure earlier in the evening. We captured the voice of an angry male spirit that whispered: "I murdered." Although we have found no historical records of a murder taking place in the home, we do believe that this house sits on the very outskirts of the original Jewish Cemetery. This would have been the unconsecrated ground where they would have buried the murderers, thieves, and anyone else unfit for a proper burial. This could also be one of the many reasons why 12 West Oglethorpe tends to be so haunted.

As the evening dwindled down and we concluded our investigation that night, we were walking through the entranceway of the home to the front door. The door swung open all of a sudden by itself. One of our investigators, David Dahlin, was a skeptic at the time and he asked: "Can you do that again?" The door then slammed shut hard enough to rattle the frame. David, sure that there must be some rational explanation, asked once again: "Can you do that once more?" Once again the door swung open on its own accord. We went to walk out, and again the door slammed shut! Now, this had to be more than just a coincidence or the wind—this door was opening and shutting on command! As we finally exited the building, one of our audio recorders captured one more EVP. A man's voice growled: "Go f**king answer the original dare." Since the house had been abandoned since 1985, the firemen in 2009 were the last living people to enter the home until our investigation in 2010. The firemen were daring each other to go to the upstairs top left bedroom, and we believe that this entity was daring us to do the exact same thing.

This home is one of the first stops on our tour, and many guests have felt the presence of this house firsthand. One child, who was about twelve years old, felt cramps in her stomach and an overall uneasy feeling as we approached the house. She was in so much pain that she was nearly doubled over but, as soon as we left the house, she was fine. She attributed her sudden malady to the house at 12 West Oglethorpe Avenue. "There is just something about that house," she muttered to her mother, "I don't like it." Many local Savannahians tend to feel the same way.

We have conducted many paranormal investigations over the years, but this is one of the few places that make me shudder when I think about it. Granted, if we were allowed to once again enter this dreadful structure and perform another investigation, we would jump at the chance. However, this is one of only two places out of our many investigations that I would rather not return to. (The other location would be the Warren A. Candler Hospital, which is located at the south end of the Historic District.)

There is an overall feeling of sadness and despair throughout the home at 12 West Oglethorpe, as well as a presence that is somewhat malevolent in nature. In addition, time itself appears to be distorted upon entering the building. You could be inside the house for five minutes, and you would come out and swear that you had been in there for two hours. There is a very real chance that this house is a rare type of haunting known as a portal haunting. It could be the threshold of a portal to the other side, where spirits can freely cross back and forth from their realm to ours. After multiple investigations of the home, we have caught evidence of numerous entities, both male and female, young and old. This supports our theory that 12 West Oglethorpe may indeed be a rare case of a portal haunting.

UNKNOWN FUTURE

No one knows how much longer this house will sit abandoned, but there are no current development plans for the property. It is now owned by the bank, and will likely remain as it is for many years to come. It is currently not for sale, and the bank has no plans for any further development on the property. The front entrance and downstairs windows are now boarded up in order to deter vagrants and amateur thrill seekers, but occasionally folks still risk the chance of getting arrested and sneak into the home. Although we don't know what will become of this historic mansion, it will still remain one of the most mysterious and haunted houses in all of Savannah.

CHAPTER 4

Voices from the Other Side
THE BOAR'S HEAD RESTAURANT INVESTIGATION

Established in 1959, the Boar's Head is one of the oldest restaurants on River Street.
Photo by Ryan Dunn

The old warehouse on River Street, which is now home to the Boar's Head Restaurant, dates back to the year 1809, when it was built for a cotton merchant named Andrew McCredie. The building now sits in what was once the Wharf Lot section of River Street, and it is one of the oldest standing structures along the Riverfront. Savannah's Great Fire of 1820, which occurred on January 11th of that year, destroyed much of the Riverfront and this structure was one of the few buildings that didn't succumb to the flames. As with almost all of the buildings on River Street, slave labor was used here to work the docks and the cotton warehouses. These unfortunate slaves lived and worked under some of the harshest conditions in the city.

In 1823, the building was sold to Andrew Low, who later went on to become one of Savannah's most prominent citizens. Low used the building for many years as the warehouse of his merchant, broker, and cotton dealing businesses. Sadly, one year after he acquired the building, on January 22, 1824, a huge fire erupted on River Street. Low's warehouse was one of many unfortunate structures destroyed by the fire. The structure was quickly rebuilt, and he continued to use the building for many more years.

Andrew Low had come to America in 1800 from Kincardinshire, Scotland, to begin a fresh start in the New World. He took up residence in Savannah and began working at a firm named Bowman Fleming, which had roots in Glasgow, Scotland. He later bought out the firm and went on to establish his own business, named Andrew Low and Company, which continued to operate successfully in Savannah for another seventy-five years. Throughout his life, however, Andrew Low never managed to get married. Busy with running his successful business, life seemed to have passed him by. As he began to age, he decided that he needed an heir to his fortune. He spoke with his eldest brother, William, in Scotland, who then sent over his seventeen-year-old son, Andrew Low II, to learn his uncle's business. The elder Andrew Low later retired in England and left the firm in his young nephew's hands.

After taking over his uncle's company, Andrew Low II later went on to become the richest man in all of Savannah. He married Sarah Cecil Hunter on January 25, 1844, and they had four children: three daughters and one son named William Mackay Low. William went on to marry Juliette Gordon, who later became famous for founding the Girl Scouts of America. The Low and the Gordon families were two of the most prominent families in Savannah at the time, and their homes are still house museums to this very day.

In 1849, Low sold the building on River Street that had housed his warehouse for many years to another shipping merchant named Lewis F. Harris. This building was then later occupied by the Willink and Marshall firm, and then the Savannah Bank and Trust Company. In the late 1890s, it became a private residence for a widow named Mrs. C.H. Daffin, who later died in the home. By the 1900s, the property was acquired by H. Solomon and Sons Warehouse, a wholesale grocers and European steamship agency. The Solomon family operated their business there for many years and, in 1959, the structure was converted into a restaurant.

A man named Jack H. Elkins purchased the old warehouse and reopened it a few months later as the Boar's Head Restaurant. Today, over fifty years later, the Boar's Head is one of the oldest operating restaurants on River Street. In 1998, Philip and Charlene Branan purchased the restaurant, where they continue to operate under the Boar's Head name. Philip, a graduate of The Culinary Institute of America in Hyde Park, New York, added his own unique twist on gourmet dishes with a southern Creole flair. The couple sources fresh vegetables from their own farm, and they quite possibly have the best shrimp and grits in all of Savannah.

In addition to being one of the best restaurants on River Street, the Boar's Head Restaurant has no shortage of ghosts.

THE HAUNTS

Not long after we established our paranormal research team, the 3-D Ghost Hunters, my wife and I were having drinks in our courtyard one evening with our next-door neighbors and good friends, Alan Gallardo and Rose Gillespie. The conversation quickly turned towards our newly established group, and Rose told us about the restaurant where she worked downtown. She had been working at the Boar's Head Restaurant for quite some time, and it was one of the most haunted restaurants on River Street.

"I can talk to the owner Charlene and see if she will let us in to investigate," mentioned Rose.

My wife and I then asked Rose to see what she could do, and less than a week later I was sitting in the dining room of the Boar's Head speaking to Charlene about the activity that occurs in the building.

FLOWER FRENZY

According to Charlene, both she and her husband, Chef Philip, had dealt with the paranormal occurrences in the old building ever since they purchased the place in 1998. As soon as they had reopened the restaurant, reports of strange occurrences began to pour in from both the customers and the employees. When they first opened, Charlene and Philip would work at the restaurant all day, from open until close. Charlene would always put fresh flowers in a small vase on every table when she came to the restaurant in the morning. When she would arrive to open the building the following morning, the flowers would be inexplicably turned over on their side. Knowing that she was the last person in the building the night before, and the first to arrive the next morning, she had no explanation for these odd occurrences.

A STRANGE MAN

One of the most common ghostly sightings at the Boar's Head concerns the far back dining room, otherwise known as the "Mermaid Room." The room gets its name from the beautiful wooden mermaid carvings that adorn its ancient walls. For many years, customers have called Charlene over to question her about a strange man that would suddenly appear at their table. As the guests were having dinner, a tall mysterious man in a long, black coat and top hat came right over to their table and then suddenly disappeared. Sightings of this man have been reported many times over the years by random customers from all over the world. The reports are always the same, and too concise to be more than just coincidence.

THE YOUNG WOMAN

Most of the paranormal activity that permeates the building, however, tends to center around the ghost of a young woman. There have been many times when Chef Philip has been the only one in the building in the morning and he has heard his name called out by a soft female voice. Other line cooks have also experienced this strange phenomenon, as well as servers and other members of the staff. It seems that this female entity is familiar with all of the employees, and she likes to call them by their names. In addition, many guests have reported hearing voices say to them: "Have a good night," as they walk out the front door, even though there is no one around them as they leave.

One early morning, a few years ago, a server knocked on the back door of the restaurant, hoping that Philip would hear him and let him in. A female voice on the other side of the door told the server to: "Go around front." After he walked in the front door of the restaurant, he realized that he and Philip were the only two people in the building. Baffled by the phantom voice, he went and spoke to Philip about what had just happened, who laughingly replied: "It must have been the ghost."

A few years ago, Charlene had a customer approach her one evening and ask: "Do you have a female ghost here?"

Charlene then replied: "Yes."

"Do you know her name?" the man asked.

Charlene then responded: "No, we do not know her name."

"Well I think her name is Laura," said the man, "and she is definitely here."

Although I could not find any evidence of the name Laura in the history of the building, this name could very well be the name of a young female slave who had died here many years before. Although we may never know, there is a female presence that continues to haunt this building nonetheless.

THE RESTROOMS

Another area of the restaurant that lends a good deal of paranormal activity are the restrooms. On many occasions, customers have come running out of the bathrooms screaming: "There's a ghost in there!" When Charlene would check on them to make sure that everything was all right, the customers would then explain that the faucets on the sinks in the restrooms began to turn on by themselves. Like many other paranormal claims at the Boar's Head Restaurant, this strange occurrence has been reported by many customers from all walks of life throughout a span of over ten years.

PONYTAIL TUG

The only physical contact with the ghosts in the building happened late one evening to a female server. She was in the Mermaid Room bussing a table when, all of a sudden, she felt a strong tug on her ponytail. Thinking that it was one of her coworkers horsing around, she spun around quickly to respond to her assailant. As she turned, she realized that no one was standing behind her, and there wasn't anyone in the vicinity who could have possibly pulled her hair. Frightened by her apparent encounter with the ghost, she raced out of the dining room.

LADY IN WHITE

Rose herself has also experienced quite a few strange encounters during her employment at the Boar's Head. One afternoon, she was in the kitchen with a fellow female server portioning out sauces. After a few minutes, the other server went upstairs to get changed for the shift. A few minutes later, Rose witnessed a female pass behind her out of the corner of her eye. The woman was wearing white, and Rose thought that it was her fellow server returning from getting dressed. A few seconds later, the server who had gone upstairs a few minutes before came walking back down the stairs. At that moment, Rose realized that she had just personally encountered the female entity that haunts the Boar's Head. ·

The Boar's Head Restaurant occupies a building built in 1809 for Andrew McCredie.
Photo by Ryan Dunn

THE INVESTIGATION

Considering the frequency of paranormal occurrences throughout the building, Charlene was very excited to have us come in and investigate to see what we could find, and she was even nice enough to give us Halloween night for the date of the investigation. After weeks of anticipation, on October 31, 2010, we arrived at the Boar's Head Restaurant with our team to begin our research. I arrived with three other investigators who were members of our team at the time: Brandon, David, and Sara Dahlin. We also had Alan and Rose join us that evening, since Rose was more familiar with the layout of the building and she had worked so hard to help gain us access to the place.

After finishing our initial readings, we split up into three teams of two and began our investigation. I was teamed up with Alan, and we began with an EVP session in the upstairs kitchen. Only five minutes into the session, we began to experience the activity in the building firsthand. The K2 EMF meter began to unexplainably light up in response to our questions, sometimes as high as 20+ milligauss! (A K2 meter is a tool that captures readings of EMF, or electromagnetic fields. Ghosts are believed to use electromagnetic energy to manifest themselves. These meters are a great way to document possible spirit activity. You do have to be careful, however, because natural power sources can cause high EMF readings as well, possibly resulting in a false reading.) We also both witnessed an unexplainable, dark shadow dart behind the coolers towards the other end of the kitchen.

The most compelling evidence of that evening's investigation, however, was caught by David and Brandon in the Mermaid Room. As both investigators were seated back-to-back in the middle of the room conducting an EVP session, they began to hear phantom footsteps all around them. The floor in the Mermaid Room is made of wood, and it sounded as if a woman in high heels was walking around the room in which they were seated. There was no one else in the room with them—at least no one else living, and the sound itself was unmistakable. A few minutes later, David heard a strange noise coming from where the video camera was placed in the room. He said to Brandon: "I'm going to get up and walk towards the camera." A moment later, a digital audio recorder that had been placed in the room earlier captured the distinct voice of a female spirit asking: "Why?" This spirit seemed to be curious as to what we were doing in the building. It seemed that we had finally made contact with the female ghost that has haunted the Boar's Head ever since Charlene and Philip bought the place in 1998.

Although we didn't capture as much evidence as we usually do on our investigations, we were able to validate the fact that the Boar's Head Restaurant was indeed haunted. In addition, we captured some very compelling evidence of the female spirit that is so often seen and heard throughout the building.

Charlene and Philip continue to operate the Boar's Head to this day, and it remains one of the best restaurants to visit while you are in Savannah. If you decide to eat there, which I highly recommend, be sure to ask for Rose; she will take excellent care of you. Also, make sure that you order their She Crab Soup, they have some of the best in town. And as for the ghosts there, they continue to make their presence known to employees and customers on an almost daily basis, so you very well may have your own personal experience with the spirits that haunt the place.

CHAPTER 5

The Haunted Hospital
THE WARREN A. CANDLER HOSPITAL INVESTIGATION

The Warren A. Candler Hospital, the second oldest hospital in the United States. *Photo by Ryan Dunn*

THE HISTORY

Located near the corners of Drayton and Gaston Streets, the abandoned Warren A. Candler Hospital has probably witnessed more tragedy and suffering than any other building in Savannah. Believed to be the second oldest general hospital in the United States, the building was constructed in 1803 as Georgia's first hospital for sick sailors and seamen. It was later renamed the Savannah Poor House and Hospital in 1808, when the building continued to be in use until the year 1818. A new building was erected a year later in 1819, and it is presently the oldest part of the hospital.

Throughout the 1800s, Savannah experienced several Yellow Fever epidemics that ravaged the entire city. The worst of these occurred in the years of 1820, 1854, and

1876. Also commonly known as *"Yellow Jack,"* and *"Bronze John,"* the virus began innocently enough with normal cold symptoms: fever, nausea, headache, and chills. The symptoms would soon subside, making the carrier believe that they were getting well. Soon after, the second phase of the virus would kick in. The sufferers would experience bleeding from the mouth and eyes, vomiting blood (hence the disease's other nickname, *"Black Vomit*)," and tongues covered in a light brown fur. The skin would then turn a jaundiced-yellow color, hence the name *"Yellow Fever."* The victim's vital organs would begin to slowly shut down one by one. They would go into a coma-like state during the final stages of the illness and, after much pain, they would eventually die. The doctors at Candler Hospital raced to fight the outbreak with outdated remedies and various medicines containing turpentine, belladonna, camphor, and arsenic. Although we now know that these attempts at a cure might have led to an even more expedient death, these desperate attempts were their only course of action. Deaths occurred everywhere at such an alarming rate that patients were often prematurely pronounced dead. They might suddenly awaken to find themselves in a coffin, six feet deep, with no one to hear their screams. At the time, Savannah's citizens had no idea that Yellow Fever was contracted by mosquitoes—it was then believed to be a communicable disease. When someone died of the fever, they were buried deep within the ground, as soon as possible, in an effort to prevent further outbreaks. Little did they know that it wasn't even a communicable disease and, in many cases, those who were pronounced dead were actually just in a weakened state due to battling the fever.

This disease was so rampant in Savannah that the cities of Charleston, Jacksonville, and Augusta enforced a mandatory seventy-two-hour quarantine for any train passenger arriving from Savannah; and Wilmington, North Carolina, banned passengers arriving from Savannah altogether. Death was everywhere. Many Savannahians fled the city in fear to escape the outbreak. The hospital realized that something had to be done to prevent mass hysteria, so an underground tunnel was created that lead from the hospital morgue to what was then an underdeveloped Forsyth Park. Under the cover of darkness, they could transport the bodies and bury the victims without alarming the citizens of the rising death toll. It is also rumored that secret rooms in the tunnel were used for autopsies and medical experiments on Yellow Fever patients. A *Savannah Morning News* article, in June of 1884, actually mentions the "dead house" of the hospital as being an "unsightly structure" with an underground system and secret autopsy rooms. In the 1990s, when the Mansion on Forsyth Park was built, only a few blocks away from the old hospital, construction workers unearthed multiple human skeletons. Could these be the bodies of the Yellow Fever victims of 1820, 1854, or 1876?

During the Civil War, the grounds of the hospital were used as Camp Davidson, a military prison for Union soldiers. When Union General William Tecumseh Sherman marched into Savannah in December of 1864, it soon changed and became a prison for confederate soldiers. The hospital was renamed the Savannah Hospital in 1872, and then changed its name yet again, in 1930, to the Warren A. Candler Hospital in honor of the Methodist Bishop. In 1980, the hospital, which is still in operation today, moved into a new facility further south of the city on Reynolds Street. The Warren A. Candler hospital building became Tidelands Community Mental Health Center in 1983, a center for

The entrance to the morgue tunnels where Yellow Fever victims' bodies were transported in the cover of night to avoid a mass hysteria. *Photo by Ryan Dunn*

substance abuse and mental health. After Tidelands left in 2000, a portion of the hospital was used as a probation and parole office until 2009. It then remained abandoned until 2012, when renovations on the old building began to become the Savannah Law School.

THE INVESTIGATION

In February of 2011, our paranormal investigation group had the privilege of investigating the Warren A. Candler hospital, which isn't something awarded to most. From the moment we arrived on the property, a heavy, malevolent, unseen presence was felt by all the investigators. Every single person that evening admitted that something didn't feel right in the building. As we walked down the dark corridors, I wondered how many had suffered in the hospital's 200-year history. We went into old surgery rooms, lined floor to ceiling with blood-stained, green-tiled walls, and we crept through chemistry labs filled with old medical equipment.

The further we went, the worse the activity became. Although there was no power to the building (except in a few remote areas), we documented readings from our Electromagnetic Field Detectors (EMF) that were off the charts. Our temperature gauges recorded unexplained significant temperature drops. After hours of investigation, the presence finally decided to reveal itself. I was walking down the hall past the patients' rooms when it happened.

As we approached the children's wing, near the old Psych Ward, the activity escalated. As two other members of our team headed down a different wing of the building, I suddenly heard the creaking of a door behind me. As I turned around to face the double door entrance of the Psych Ward, I noticed that the door on the left was wide open. Now this feat is not easily explained, because these doors required a latch to be turned before they can open. As soon as I laid eyes on it, the door slammed shut with a tremendous force. This door also has a spring hinge on it, which helps it to slowly close; so for this door to be slammed shut as hard as it did would require an uncanny amount of strength, and my team was nowhere near this door.

A few minutes before this incident, I had been taking snapshots of the interior of the hospital for our records. Luckily, I still had my camera in tow when it happened. As fast as my finger could reach the flash, I snapped a picture down the hallway. In the photo you can clearly see what appears to be a female entity looking back at me through the window on the left door. Judging by the look on her face, she does not seem at all happy with our presence. Throughout the entire investigation, we had the intense feeling of being watched, and this photo was proof.

The apparition of a female face can be seen in the left window of the door to the women and children's psychiatric ward of the hospital. *Photo by Ryan Dunn*

In addition to the photo, we captured some great Class A EVPs as well. In the hallway, we caught a male entity on recording who told us to: "Get out." In the morgue tunnels, as we approached a doorway that had been bricked up, we caught an EVP that told us to: "Bash it." One of the most compelling EVPs captured in the morgue tunnels was a conversation between two entities. A female voice says: "I have Zach on my charts." A male spirit then replies: "Get out of the room, I'm working." Could this be a conversation between a nurse and doctor concerning a patient? Maybe this piece of evidence is proof that the underground tunnels were indeed used for medical experiments and autopsies during the height of Savannah's Yellow Fever epidemics.

HOME

From the moment we arrived home after the investigation, it was apparent that something wasn't right. We had brought something back with us. The unsettling feeling we experienced as we had entered the hospital returned. My wife and I, as well as my two young daughters, became unexplainably sick. As we lay in bed at night, we could hear people talking in our hallway, although no one was there. Also, the overall feeling of being watched was more than apparent. Noises from our attic were so loud, it sounded as if someone was moving furniture up there.

Our other investigators present at the Candler Hospital investigation, David and Brandon Dahlin, were living in Atlanta at that time. We had not spoken since the investigation, and then Brandon called me the following day. The first thing out of his mouth was: "I think we brought something home with us." My heart sank. He was experiencing the same activity at his home, four hours away!

After about a week or so, I woke up one morning and realized that the presence I'd felt was no longer in the house. Whatever had attached itself to us had finally decided to let up. This was not the first time that we had brought our work home with us, but it was definitely the most unsettling experience we have ever had. Whatever paranormal presence is at the old hospital is very possessive over its domain. Should you ever decide to visit the Old Candler Hospital, be sure that you are alone when you leave.

DON'T BRING THEM HOME!

In our work, there is always the possibility of bringing spirit attachments back home with you. To begin with, I always say a prayer of protection before entering any haunted location. In addition, Kim and I regularly use Holy Water and natural sea salts around the doorways and windows of our home to prevent negative entities from entering. Smudging with sticks of sage is also a great way to keep your house free of negative entities. Prevention is always better than a cure.

OTHERS EXPERIENCE THE HOSPITAL

A few years after the investigation, in fall of 2013, I had the pleasure of meeting Christine Michaels, who used to work at the old hospital from November of 2005 until November of 2008. In the 2000s, the old section of the hospital was used as a probation and parole office, and she was a probation officer there. Throughout her years of working at Candler, Christine had numerous unexplainable paranormal experiences. Her office was located in the basement of the old building, just around the corner from the old morgue. There were many times that she spent late hours working in the building alone, after everyone else had left for the day.

As Christine would finish up her paperwork late in the evening, she would hear strange sounds throughout the building—even in the hallway right outside her office door. There was the unmistakable sound of scratching and voices heard in her office all around her, although the words were just low enough to not be heard. It sounded as if full conversations were happening all around her, though she was the only one in the building. When she would speak about it to her coworkers the following day, it was apparent that they had experienced some of the same activity, although they were too frightened to talk about the strange occurrences. It seemed as if they felt that talking about the paranormal activity in the building would stir it up even more. There were also numerous instances where alarms would be triggered when Christine was the only one in the building. Phantom footsteps were often heard walking down the hallways, especially right near the old morgue. It seemed apparent that many of the people who had died there over the hospital's many dismal years still continued to haunt the place.

Although very interested in the subject, it wasn't until a few years later that Christine became a paranormal investigator herself. Her team, Ghost Hunt Weekends, has conducted many successful investigations themselves. Her encounters with the paranormal at Candler Hospital may have been just the beginning, but they were unforgettable experiences nonetheless.

The Warren A. Candler Hospital is one of the most coveted haunted locations in Savannah's Historic District. Since our investigation of the place, the structure has undergone major renovations to convert it into the Savannah Law School. Construction still continues on the building today to try and restore it to its original splendor. Although renovations tend to stir up paranormal activity in a building, perhaps the restoration of the old hospital will finally put these tormented souls to rest. It may remain dormant for now, but only time will tell.

CHAPTER 6
Messages from Beyond
THE AMETHYST INN
INVESTIGATION

The Amethyst Inn, built in 1888 for Tomlinson Fort Johnson. *Photo by Ryan Dunn*

Just south of Whitefield Square, at the corner of Gaston and Habersham Streets, lies the majestic Amethyst Inn. A beautiful example of early Victorian architecture, the Amethyst Inn, with its vibrant shades of purple and white, complete with gingerbread trim, resembles something out of a fairy tale. The current owners, Rocky and Jane Reed, along with their daughter Sarah, have resided in the home, where they have been operating their bed and breakfast since the late 1990s. The Reeds have fully restored the home to its original splendor, along with becoming one of the top B&Bs in the city of Savannah. They, along with their guests, began to experience paranormal activity in the home soon after they moved in.

THE HISTORY

The Amethyst Inn, located at 402 East Gaston Street, was built in 1888 for a man named Tomlinson Fort Johnson. Throughout his years, Johnson was the manager of the Savannah Theatre, a collector for the U.S. Customs office, and he was also the proprietor of the Planter's Hotel, which is now the Planter's Inn on Reynolds Square. He lived at his home on Gaston Street until the year 1900, when the home became the prestigious Hartridge School for Girls, a private prep school run by Miss E.B. Hartridge. In 1907, the property once again became a private residence when John Cooper Harris moved into the home with his family. He passed away there a few years later, and may very well be one of the inn's resident ghosts. The property then changed hands numerous times, and there were a few other deaths in the home, although most were from natural causes.

In the 1940s, however, there was one documented death that did occur in the home that was not from natural causes. In an upstairs bedroom, that is now the Dahlia Room, a young man named B.F. Skinner took his own life. When his body was discovered, he was found hanging on the back of the door with a makeshift noose tied around his neck. This could shed some light as to why the Dahlia Room is still one of the most haunted rooms in the old inn.

From the 1960s to the 1990s, the house was divided into five separate apartments, with numerous tenants living there over the years. It became the Amethyst Inn Bed and Breakfast in the late 1990s and remains so to this day. The inn, which offers eight fully restored suites complete with period antique furnishings, has experienced paranormal activity in almost every room since its opening.

THE HAUNTS

Guests have been locked in their rooms on multiple occasions, with no rational explanation, and doors tend to lock by themselves when no one else is around. Although there seems to be a playful spirit at large in the old inn, there is a darker entity that may reside there as well.

THE ROSE ROOM

In the Rose Room, for instance, a female guest staying at the inn awoke in the middle of the night to the frightening sensation of some unseen presence lightly brushing across her arm. She recalled being soothed by the spectral touch, but then reported hearing phantom footsteps pacing back and forth soon after. The sound was coming from upstairs, although there was no one staying in the room above her on that particular night.

THE DAHLIA ROOM

The Dahlia Room tends to be one of the most active rooms in the house. A couple was staying in the room one night a few years ago, and the woman, from Jamaica, was sensitive to the spirit world. At around midnight, she had experienced all that she could handle, and they left the inn in the middle of the night. She explained to Jane, the owner of the inn that the reason for their leaving was because the house needed a cleansing, and that it was haunted by multiple spirits. The woman could not rest due to all of the paranormal activity in the building. This could very well be true, because we were able to capture evidence of multiple entities during our investigation there.

On another occasion, a female guest went to bed one night in the Dahlia Room. When she awoke the next morning, she discovered a strange antique tube of lipstick on the nightstand beside the bed. No one else had been in the room all night, and she could not explain how it had gotten there.

This phenomenon, known as "apportation," occurs when an object crosses over into our realm from the spirit world. These objects usually tend to be personal belongings of the deceased, and in many cases antiques. This phenomenon is very rare, but it has been known to occur from time to time. This is the same room in which Jane's daughter, Sarah, would lead her friends to when she was a small child. She would explain to them that they were going there to meet "Casper." Evidently, Sarah would converse with the ghost of a small boy in that room on occasion. For lack of a better name, she had nicknamed the little boy "Casper."

This, however, was not Sarah Reed's only experience with the ghosts there. When she was younger, both she and her older sister would often see the apparition of a male soldier walking up and down the main stairway that leads to the second floor.

THE HYDRANGEA SUITE

In the Hydrangea Suite, a female guest staying there one evening with her infant child had a strange encounter with the entities that haunt the inn. The mother had her infant strapped into a high chair in the front room, and she had walked into the kitchenette to fix a baby bottle, when her child suddenly started crying. She went back into the front room to grab the baby's pacifier, which she had left on a table all the way across the room from where the infant was seated. As she entered the room, the child stopped crying, and the pacifier was in the child's mouth. The mother could find no logical explanation for what had just happened, so she reported the incident to Jane, who explained to the woman that the inn did have its fair share of resident ghosts.

A FRIENDLY GHOST

In the early 1990s, before it became the Amethyst Inn and the home was still split into separate apartments, a man by the name of Jack Richards lived there. Jack is the original creator of *Ghost Walks Ghost Talks*, one of the oldest walking ghost tours in the city of Savannah. One afternoon, Jack was downstairs at a friend's apartment, which is now Jane and Rocky Reed's bedroom. He suddenly witnessed the apparition of a man standing by the fireplace. The man was wearing overalls and a plaid shirt, and seemed to Jack to be of a friendly nature. After a few seconds, the apparition suddenly disappeared.

"I realized that I had just seen a ghost," exclaimed Jack to me over the phone during a brief interview. "He seemed friendly," finished Jack, "but he was not shy about letting me see him, that's for sure!"

THE INVESTIGATION

In February of 2011, we were contacted by Jane Reed regarding the paranormal activity surrounding the Amethyst Inn. I briefly spoke with her over the phone and we set up an interview in person at the inn for the following week. It didn't take long to realize that these occurrences had been going on for quite some time. Jane told me about all of the incidents occurring with her guests over the years, as well as with her and her family. She spoke about shadow people seen out of the corners of her eyes and peripheral visions that occurred quite often throughout the home. It was not a rare occurrence to see a dark shadow dart past for just a moment. She even told me about how the playful spirits liked to pull small "pranks" around the house, especially on Rocky. The doorbell would ring and no one would be outside when Jane answered the door. Lights would unexplainably turn on and off by themselves, doors would mysteriously lock without assistance, and, on more than one occasion, guests would leave in the middle of the night due to all of the activity.

We set up an investigation for February 22, 2011, at which time we were given the full run of the home to conduct our research.

Even before our investigation began, the activity in the home started up. At the beginning of every investigation, we record base readings of relative humidity, temperature, electromagnetic fields, and negative and positive ions. This way, if we have a fluctuation during our investigation, we have something to base it against. We had five investigators present that evening (Brandon, David, and Sara Dahlin, as well as my wife Kim, and me).

As we were doing initial sweeps throughout the home, we captured two very interesting EVPs on our digital voice recorders. In the basement, in Sarah's bedroom, we caught a very high EMF (electromagnetic field) spike on our K2 EMF detector that we could not explain that registered over 20 milligauss. At the same time, one of our digital audio recorders in the room caught an EVP of a male spirit that whispered: "Sarah."

A few minutes later, we split up into two teams: one team of three investigators and one team of two investigators. The team of three headed up to the second floor to the Dahlia Room, while the team of two remained in the basement, two floors apart. All of a sudden, both teams heard a loud, unexplainable crash, and the second-floor team radioed the basement team on the walkie talkie.

"What was that?" I asked Brandon, who was in the basement with Kim.

"I don't know," he replied, "but it sounded like it was down here with us."

At that same moment, Brandon's digital voice recorder captured the voice of a male entity that replied: "It was."

One of the most compelling pieces of audio evidence was captured later that evening on the stairwell in the main entranceway. Kim and Brandon were conducting an EVP session on the stairway, when she asked: "Who is the apparition that keeps appearing in all of the photos?"

A female spirit answered: "Go ask Cooper."

According to historical records, John Cooper Harris lived at 402 East Gaston Street with his wife and children in the year 1907. Since one of his sons was a junior, he went by the name of "Cooper." This is the same stairway where Sarah and her sister would often see the apparition of a male soldier when they were younger.

NATURAL EXPLANATIONS

Although we were able to prove that the Amethyst Inn is indeed haunted by multiple ghosts, we found a few other natural explanations for some of the phenomena there. For instance, we were able to explain the ringing of the doorbell that is so often experienced. It turns out that when Jane's neighbors used their garage door openers, the sensor in the doorbell would be triggered, which made it ring when no one was outside the door. Although we are paranormal investigators, a paranormal explanation is always our last resort. We may have been able to debunk this phenomenon, but we were not able to explain everything else we captured during our investigation of the old inn.

ENERGY DRAIN

In addition to capturing some great audio evidence during our investigation, we also found strange anomalies in our temperature and EMF readings, as well as a few personal experiences to boot. While in the Rose Room during an EVP session, Sara and I became completely drained of energy and exhausted for no explainable reason. The next moment, a strange, bright white light appeared from under the door leading to the hallway. Sara shined her flashlight at the odd glowing light, and it suddenly disappeared. There was no one outside the door and, the other team was on another floor of the building. As soon as Sara and I left the room, we both felt as if a heavy pressure had been lifted off of us. The feeling of being drained of all of our energy had passed as quickly as it had come. I believe that whatever it was, the entity had used our energy in the Rose Room to manifest itself, especially since we became drained right before we witnessed the unexplainable light phenomena.

To this day, the Reeds and their guests deal with paranormal phenomena on a regular basis. Whether it is shadow people passing through the hallway or a guest unexplainably trapped in a locked bedroom, the ghosts of the Amethyst Inn will most likely continue to haunt this place for many years to come.

Should you ever decide to come and visit our beautiful city, be sure to book a room here, at least for one evening. One night may be more than enough, if you are not used to sharing your room with ghosts. The Reeds are a wonderful family and excellent hosts, and they operate one of the most beautiful bed and breakfasts in America. Be sure, however, to keep a watchful eye, because you may very well have at least one extra guest with you that you may not have expected.

CHAPTER 7

A Poltergeist on River Street
THE CHART HOUSE RESTAURANT INVESTIGATION

The Chart House Restaurant, nestled in one of the oldest masonry structures in the whole state of Georgia. *Photo by Ryan Reese*

THE HISTORY

The Chart House Restaurant, which uniquely manages to front both Bay and River Streets, is one of the oldest standing buildings in the city of Savannah. This building is also considered by many to be the oldest existing masonry structure in the entire State of Georgia. The building itself was built on a lot purchased by a man named Captain John Taylor in the year 1791 for 750 pounds of sterling silver. A two-story structure was built the following year in 1792 as his private residence, and the top two floors of the building were later added in the year 1818 by his son, William Taylor. In the late 1800s, the building was converted into both a produce store and a saloon, which, oddly enough, conducted business during the same hours. Only in a city like Savannah could you shop for groceries and grab a cocktail at the same time.

A fire burned part of the home many years later in 1885, but the structure was then quickly rebuilt. It later went on to become a cotton warehouse, the Savannah Ship Chandlery, the Southern Marine Supply Company, and the Bethel Air Conditioning Company over the many years of its existence. In 1979, the Chart House Restaurant purchased the historic building and turned it into one of the best high-end restaurants in Savannah. Although we did find records of deaths occurring in the home over the years, all appeared to be of natural causes. Due to the location on River Street and the age of the building, however, we did find records that many slaves were kept there in extremely harsh conditions. This could possibly account for some of the paranormal activity that continues to permeate throughout the entire building, even to this very day.

In March of 2011, I was contacted by the Chart House concerning multiple paranormal encounters throughout the building. I met with Billy Kitchens, the general manager, who told me during an interview about everything going on there. I sat and listened as he discussed, in great detail, the odd occurrences surrounding the Chart House Restaurant. There were firsthand reports dating back to 1979 from former employees when it first opened. During that year, there were five employees hanging out after the restaurant closed one evening on the main floor. They were standing around talking, when the apparition of a little girl in a white dress ran quickly past them and into the women's restroom. Shocked with terror at what they had just witnessed, all five employees abruptly left the building.

RENOVATIONS

According to Billy, the paranormal activity in the building would always increase quite a bit when they would attempt to remodel the historic structure. I then explained to him that we encounter this problem quite often in our line of work. We have come to realize that ghosts do not like renovations at all, and, apparently, this was true at the Chart House as well. During one remodeling, one whole construction crew abruptly quit after the majority of them witnessed a female apparition in period dress that moved by them while they were working one afternoon in the second floor dining room. The apparition quickly passed through the restaurant and then continued to disappear into the wall. During the last renovation, a crew was hanging a huge chandelier in the middle of the restaurant when, all of a sudden, it came crashing down to the ground. They could not explain what had caused the incident, because they had rigged a support cable to prevent this from happening.

OTHER PARANORMAL EVENTS

Employees and guests alike have reported the uneasy feeling of being watched, as well as the feeling of someone near them, even when they think they are alone. On numerous occasions, employees hear their names called out when no one else is around. In addition, they often hear heavy footsteps pacing back and forth on the upper floors after closing up, although they are the only ones left in the building. There have even been reports of hearing phantom footsteps on the stairs and seeing the banister move from side to side, as if grasped by invisible hands. More than once, servers have been spooked by the feeling of some ominous presence brushing past them, leaving a disturbing cold chill behind.

A STRANGE WOMAN AND BLUE MAN

On three separate occasions, guests have reported seeing the apparition of a young woman in a lacy, long, white antique dress disappear into the wall. This has occurred on both the second and the third floor dining areas facing the river. All of the guests who have witnessed this apparition have described the same woman, and these incidents have occurred months apart. One night, a female employee was having dinner in the second floor dining room facing the river with her roommate and her roommate's son, who was then almost three years old. During dinner, the child suddenly announced that he was "scared of the blue man standing behind the lady." He became so distraught that they had to have the rest of their dinner boxed up to go.

THE SUPPLY CLOSET

One morning, at around six o'clock, Rob Britton, the executive chef, was performing his usual daily opening duties. All of a sudden, he heard a strange tapping noise on the cooler glass in the kitchen. He went over to the cooler to investigate the noise, and he was frozen with fright, as he witnessed a smoky form manifest itself into the shape of a ball and then suddenly dart out of the doorway. As it went rushing into the hallway, a binder hanging on the wall started swinging by itself, as if the form had brushed past it. Soon afterwards, Rob and another chef, who were the only ones in the building at that time, heard a loud commotion coming from the fourth floor. The sound was coming from the supply closet, and it sounded as if someone was tearing the place apart. Rob immediately called Billy, who was due in a few hours later at around eight o'clock in the morning.

When Billy finally arrived, the three men reluctantly headed upstairs to the fourth floor. As Billy opened the door to the supply closet, all three men were amazed at what they saw. Everything on the shelves had been thrown to the floor and the room was a complete disaster. Billy decided that they should finish the opening duties, and then focus on the mess at hand. He closed the door to the supply closet, and the three men returned about an hour later to clean up the mess. When Billy opened the door this time, the sight was even more astounding. Everything on the floor had been stacked up symmetrically on the back wall of the supply closet. No one could explain what they had just witnessed.

We call this type of activity poltergeist activity. The word "poltergeist" comes from the German language and means "noisy ghost" or "noisy spirit." This term is a very general term used to describe paranormal activity in which objects are mysteriously moved about, or when unexplainable loud rapping or tapping noises occur. In most cases, poltergeists are centered around teenagers and they possibly may not even be ghosts at all, but energy dispelled by someone in angst about going through the changes of life. In other cases, however, like this one, poltergeists are indeed powerful spirits who are able to manifest enough energy to make objects move about—seemingly on their own accord.

A FOURTH FLOOR APPARITION

A few months later, Rob had another encounter with the ghosts of the old Chart House. He recalls having a very uncomfortable feeling one morning about going up to the fourth floor. As he was opening up that morning, he completed all of his other duties first, and put off going to the fourth floor until the very last. At around 10:30 that morning, after he had completed everything else, he finally had to head up to the fourth floor. As he made his way up the last few steps, his stomach was in knots. He slowly opened the door to a disturbing sight. A few feet before him stood a full-figure apparition of a male entity. The spirit locked eyes with Rob and glared at him intently, and then stepped back a few steps and quickly disappeared. Something inside had told him not to go to the fourth floor, and now he had actually seen the ghost! This was not the first time, and it would definitely not be his last encounter with the ghosts that haunt this building.

THE INVESTIGATION

After listening to all of these encounters about the ghosts that seemed to reside there from Billy, we both agreed that a full paranormal investigation was a necessity. On April 3rd, we arrived at the Chart House at around 10:30 p.m. to set up for that night's investigation. The night was still and quiet, which worked out greatly in our favor. It wasn't long after arriving to the site that the spirits made contact.

THE LITTLE GIRL

I was walking through the kitchen on the second floor, getting initial readings of temperature, humidity, and electromagnetic fields. I always have my digital recorder running during an investigation, and I was dictating readings into my recorder, when I managed to capture an EVP of a small, young girl. She appeared to be interested in the equipment I was using, because she asked in a small quiet voice: "Can I play?" With this piece of evidence being captured so early into the night, we were in for a very eventful investigation.

VIBRATIONS AND EMF READINGS

Later on in the evening, while we were headed up the staircase to the third floor, another investigator and I had a very chilling encounter. We noticed that the handrail on the stairs was vibrating, as if someone were holding on to it while going up the staircase. We both froze instantly and paused to listen and began to hear the same phantom footsteps that Billy had described to me only a few days before, during our interview. After a few moments, the phenomena stopped just as suddenly as it had begun. There was no one else on the stairs, and we had no way to explain what we had just witnessed.

It took us a few moments to collect our thoughts after the incident on the stairs, but we finally made it to the third floor. We decided to sit down at a table with a window looking out to an area near the river and conduct an EVP session to see if we could get some spirit voices on audio recording. During the session, I pulled out my K2 EMF meter to try to get some fluctuations with EMF fields in order to back up our data. I asked for the spirit in the room to light up my K2 meter if it was present. We then suddenly received an EMF spike of 20 milligauss, which is rather high. Throughout this particular session, we did not catch any EVPs, but we were able to document EMF spikes that were off the charts and seemed to be in response to our questions. This occurred for the next fifteen minutes, and we could not find any natural explanation for the frequent EMF fluctuations. During this same session, we were also able to document a sudden five-degree temperature drop from 71°F to 66°F that we could not readily explain.

DREADED FOURTH FLOOR

We later decided to venture to the fourth floor, even though everyone was somewhat apprehensive, due to the stories that surrounded it. Although we were a bit reluctant, we were also excited, because this seemed to be one of the most haunted areas of the restaurant. We weren't sure what to expect, but we had a feeling that this might be where we would catch the bulk of our evidence that evening. During an EVP session in the fourth floor supply closet, I and two other investigators experienced the poltergeist activity firsthand. I was conducting an EVP session there with David and Brandon Dahlin when it happened.

We were in the closet and the lights were off, but we were armed with a night vision video camera and three digital recorders. I asked: "Can you make a really loud noise and let us know that you are here?" Immediately after asking the question, there was a noise so loud that it sounded as if someone had just punched through a wall. All three of us scrambled to the door as fast as we could. I turned the light on, and there was nothing out of place. We spent the next ten minutes scouring over the closet, only to find no rational explanation for our encounter. This was not, however, our last experience with the paranormal activity on the fourth floor.

Later in the evening, as my team was on the second floor, Kim's team was on the fourth floor conducting an EVP session. Sara Dahlin came rushing down the stairs and exclaimed: "You guys have to get up here and check this out!"

We sped up the stairs as fast as we could to see what was going on. The area in question was an electrical/equipment closet located on the fourth floor.

"Watch this," said Kim with delight in her voice. "Can you make that noise for us again?"

All of a sudden, there was this rhythmic tapping response that occurred repeatedly for over three minutes. We started looking about the room to see if we could find a logical explanation for this noise, but we could find none.

I sent one of our investigators to go and grab Billy from downstairs—he had to be here for this.

"What's going on?" asked Billy, as he walked through the door only a few minutes later.

We quickly brought him up to speed and he listened to the noise.

After about five minutes of searching about, he said, "I know this restaurant inside and out. That's not the air handler, pipes, or anything else. I don't know what it is, but I can't explain it, and it's in response to your questions."

Overall, the phenomena occurred off and on for about 20 minutes, but, to this day, we still can't figure out the cause of it.

Throughout the night, the spirits of the Chart House continued to cause more and more activity. At about four o'clock in the morning, we finally started to wrap things up. We thanked Billy for allowing us access to the restaurant for our investigation, and he told us that we were the first group to ever investigate this building, and as of today, we still are. We felt honored to have this distinct privilege, and said thank you yet again as we said our goodbyes.

As I pulled out of the parking garage, my phone started ringing; it was Billy. "You are not going to believe this," he shouted, "but it sounds as if people are running back and forth on the fourth floor. It's so loud! I guess you guys really stirred things up!"

When we had left a few minutes before, Billy was the only one still in the building. He quickly locked up and went home.

If you are ever near River Street, I highly recommend the Chart House. Ask for a table by the window overlooking the River, if there is one available, but keep an open mind. You never know what you may experience while having dinner there, so be prepared to have a possible encounter with the paranormal.

If you are worried about running into a ghost, you may want to venture outside of the Historic District for dinner. Almost everything downtown is haunted—the Chart House just happens to be one of the most haunted of all.

CHAPTER 8

The Great Houdini
BRADLEY'S LOCK AND KEY
INVESTIGATION

The Bradley family has been fixing locks here for over 100 years. *Photo by Ryan Dunn*

The Bradley's have had close ties to the Houdini family for many years. *Photo by Ryan Dunn*

THE HISTORY

Tucked away in the northeast corner of Wright Square, the Bradley's Locksmith and Key shop (now known as Bradley's Lock and Key) has served the citizens of Savannah for over 100 years. The building, which is located at 24 East State Street, was originally built in the year 1855 for Patrick Duffy. The property itself changed hands a few times over the years, as well as becoming a boarding house, before it was finally purchased by Simon Bradley in 1902. Bradley moved his family business from across the street, which had been open there since 1883. Ever since 1902, however, this building has remained virtually unchanged. It was originally opened as an umbrella repair shop called Southern Umbrella Works, but later evolved into a locksmith shop known as Bradley's Locksmith and Key, which still remains to this day. From one generation to the next, father to son, the Bradley family has carried on their family business.

The current owner of Bradley's Lock and Key is William Houdini Bradley, who affectionately goes by the nickname "Dini" to all of his friends and family. Dini Bradley was named after Harry Houdini, because his father, Aaron Bradley, was very close friends with the infamous magician and his wife many years ago. It is even rumored that Aaron Bradley may have also designed some of the famed magician's original locks and safes used in his stunning acts. Not only was he a great locksmith, but Aaron Bradley was also a noted spiritualist and medium in his day—so much so, that when Harry Houdini died a few years later, Aaron performed multiple séances for Mrs. Houdini to try to speak with her late husband. After several attempts, however, they were unable to contact the dead magician. According to Aaron Bradley, Houdini had most likely already crossed over to the other side. We do believe that Bradley was not a fake, otherwise he would have made something up to pacify Houdini's grieving wife, Bess. Oddly enough, the connection between the Houdinis and the Bradleys does run a bit deeper. Harry Houdini briefly apprenticed as a locksmith for a short time before he finally entered the world of magic.

Throughout his life, Harry Houdini was always a skeptic of the paranormal, but he did have a keen interest in the subject and wanted proof. He used to regularly attend séances when he was alive, in the hopes that he might have an encounter with the supernatural. On most occasions, however, he was disappointed. Due to the fact that Houdini was so great with sleight of hand and illusion, he was able to figure out various mediums' tricks and discounted them as charlatans. Houdini spent much of his life debunking many famous mediums. Although Houdini didn't share his good friend, Sir Arthur Conan Doyle's belief in the spiritual world, he still wished to find some evidence of life after death. Years before he died, he had hoped that the supernatural existed. Houdini and his wife made a special pact. Whoever died first, the other one would try to contact the other through the means of a séance. They supposedly created a code word in order to avoid any trickery on behalf of the medium. Magicians and researchers alike have debated for many years as to the existence of this secret password, but no one knows for sure what it was, or even if it indeed existed at all.

When Harry died first, unexpectedly on October 31, 1926, his wife vowed to try to contact her dead husband. For many years, she would hold a séance on Halloween, the anniversary of his death, to try to communicate with him. She even offered up a $10,000 reward to anyone who could provide her with a valid message from her husband on the other side. Unfortunately, the grief-stricken Mrs. Houdini never heard this code word relayed to her during any of the séances after her husband passed away. She spent much of her last years hoping that Harry would somehow contact her, but to no avail.

MILTON

Although the close ties to the Houdini family are one very interesting aspect of the Bradley family, this still doesn't account for the hauntings that have occurred over the years in the building. Years ago, Dini Bradley had an older brother named Milton. Although the name Milton Bradley is often connected with the famous board-game mogul, this isn't the same person. This similarity just happens to be purely coincidental. Milton was a war hero during World War II, and he had served in the Pacific with the United States Navy. He suffered a shrapnel wound to the head, after he tried to save the remains of a fallen comrade. The soldier had been blown apart, and Milton was trying to use his helmet in order to gather his companion's remains when he was suddenly struck in the head by a shell.

The ship that Milton was serving on was then destroyed by enemy fire, leaving him to cling to a life raft for days in the ocean before he was discovered. When he was finally rescued, he was dehydrated, malnourished, and riddled with sores. His skin was blistered with sunburn, and he looked like a human skeleton. It was a miracle that Milton was even alive. He was quickly rushed to a hospital in the Pacific, where he was quickly treated and later transferred to a hospital in Texas. While in Texas, Milton could not even recall who he was or what had happened to him during the attack on his ship. He had no identification and no dog tags, so the doctors had no way of discovering who this man really was. A few days later, by pure chance, a doctor from Savannah, who was stationed in Texas, happened to recognize Milton and was able to clear up the matter. Milton was finally able to go home, but even after this horrific ordeal, his nightmare had just begun.

Not long after returning home, Milton Bradley received a full frontal lobotomy. The atrocities that he had suffered during the war had left him indignant. Sadly enough, in those days, this was the way that these types of situations were handled. The lobotomy left Milton feeble in mind, so his younger brother, Dini, became his caretaker and would look after him during the day. Milton would mill about around Wright Square while Dini ran the shop. According to Dini, Milton was a very kind and giving man. He was the type of guy who would even give you the coat off of his back. Dini had to give Milton an allowance, because he would give every bit of his money to the first person who asked for some spare change. Many years later, one fateful afternoon, Milton Bradley met someone who would drastically change his life forever.

In April of 1994, Milton Bradley met Gary Ray Bowles. Bowles, who was a drifter, quickly befriended the 72-year-old man. He allowed Bowles to stay at his house, since he had an extra bedroom. Little did Milton know, however, that he was in the presence

Bradley's Lock and Key fixes almost anything, with only a few exceptions.
Photo by Ryan Dunn

of a violent serial killer who had already killed two victims before arriving in Savannah.

On May 5, 1994, the groundskeeper at the Savannah Golf Club discovered Milton's body while making his morning rounds. He was behind a shed, and he had been severely beaten and then strangled to death. His mouth had been stuffed with leaves and dirt, and his hands were bruised, this showing signs of a struggle. It wasn't long before they connected his murder to Gary Ray Bowles.

The television show *America's Most Wanted* filmed an episode about Gary Ray Bowles in July of 1994, which included Bradley's Lock and Key, in the hopes of catching him. Before Bowles was finally apprehended on October 22, 1994 in Jacksonville, Florida, he had managed to kill a total of six victims, as well as end up on the FBI's Top 10 Most Wanted list a week before he was captured.

THE INVESTIGATION

Kim and I approached Dini Bradley in the summer of 2011 about conducting a paranormal investigation at Bradley's Lock and Key shop. For years, we had heard all of the local ghost stories surrounding the old shop, and we were curious to see what our team might find there should we be afforded the opportunity to investigate. As we walked down State Street that sunny afternoon, we were astounded as we approached the shop. There was a hand-painted sign outside of the building which read: "We fix anything but a broken heart, we sharpen anything but your wits." The windows themselves were filled with all kinds of oddities and curiosities, and the shop itself was filled to the brim with all kinds of other unique items. From mini cannons to antique cash registers, Bradley's Lock and Key had it all. As I stepped into the place, I felt as if I had stepped back in time. The walls were lined with thousands of keys of various shapes and sizes, and the tables were littered with tools. It seemed that the place was part lock shop, part museum. The building was filled with an infinite multitude of wonders.

As we approached Mr. Bradley, in my mind I was rehearsing how I would bring up the sensitive subject of ghosts, especially considering the tragic past of his brother, Milton. As we walked up to the man, his first words to us were: "Ghosts? Of course we have ghosts. We've had ghosts in this building for years!"

I was surprised at how open he was about the fact that his building was haunted. I was even more astonished at how Mr. Bradley knew the reason for our visit before I even opened my mouth. All in all, the introduction went a lot better than I thought it would. Mr. Bradley proceeded to tell me about his family's close ties with the Harry Houdini family, as well as about the supernatural phenomena that surrounded the old building. After speaking with him for a few minutes, he readily agreed to allow us to come in at a later date and investigate the place.

On June 18, 2011, the day had finally come, and our team arrived at Bradley's Lock and Key to conduct our research. Since the building was smaller, we chose to go with a team of four investigators, as well as with Adam Van Brimmer, an editor for the *Savannah Morning News*. Van Brimmer was doing a story on our paranormal research team and wanted to experience an investigation firsthand.

EVPS

As we began our initial readings, I already had a strange feeling about the place. Although it was a unique shop, the place frankly gave us all the creeps. As we were getting readings in the back supply room, one of our full-spectrum video cameras, all of a sudden, powered down unexplainably. Although the camera had been fully charged prior to arrival, we could not even get it to turn back on. The camera did not work again properly until hours later, after we had left the site of the investigation. At that same moment, my digital recorder captured an EVP of a male spirit whispering: "Help me." Later on in the investigation, we capture that same spirit's voice in the same room, but this time he says: "Get off me." Could this be the residual ghost of Milton Bradley replaying his attack from Gary Ray Bowles? This is only speculation, but it could also be one possibility.

Another disturbing EVP was captured in the back room of the shop. During an EVP session, I asked: "Were you in the Civil War?" A male spirit then clearly replied "Dig." I do not know why the entity was asking us to dig, but with multiple cemeteries now under many of the streets in Savannah's Historic District, I could only imagine what this entity was referring to. In addition, Bradley's Locksmith and Key is just off of the northeast corner of Wright Square, where public executions took place for many years during the early years of Savannah's existence.

We also managed to catch an EVP in the middle room on a static recorder left on a table there. As all four investigators, along with Van Brimmer, reentered the room, the recorder captured the voice of a female spirit that said: "Hide, go, get away." I'm still not sure to this day whether the entity was speaking to us or possibly speaking to another spirit in the room. It sounded to me as if the entity was warning other spirits to hide from us. Either way, we were definitely capturing compelling evidence of the paranormal during our investigation of Bradley's Lock and Key.

A few hours later, we started to wrap things up and pack up our equipment. Before we left, I strolled through the old shop, marveling at all of the hidden treasures that Bradley's had to offer. I spoke with Van Brimmer, and answered any questions that he had concerning our investigation and our upcoming article. As we left, we thanked Mr. Bradley for his time and for allowing us access to his shop. As soon as I walked out of the front door of the place, I felt as if a huge weight had been lifted off of my shoulders. That uncomfortable feeling in the pit of my stomach that I had had since we arrived suddenly went away. I was glad to finally be out of that building and back into the open, summer air.

The following week, Adam Van Brimmer's article on our team and the Bradley's Lock and Key shop made front page of the *Savannah Morning News*. He did a great job detailing not only our group and the old lock shop investigation, but also the Amethyst Inn investigation that we had just completed that spring as well. The article spawned local interest in our team, and the calls began to come in at an alarming rate. Now that Savannah knew that there was someone in town who handled paranormal cases, the private-residence calls also began to pour in.

I always try to make a stop by Bradley's Lock and Key on our ghost tours, and I always encourage our patrons to return sometime during the day while they are in town to have a key made. Dini Bradley is one of the most interesting individuals I have ever met. He will tell you stories of how his father knew Harry Houdini well and of his father's unique gift of being able to commune with the dead. Bradley's is definitely a must see while you are in our unique city. If you are from Savannah, however, then you are most likely already familiar with the old lock shop and the family. In either case, keep an eye out for Milton, who is quite possibly still lurking around the old shop to this very day.

CHAPTER 9

Spirits of Another Kind
THE MOON RIVER BREWING COMPANY INVESTIGATION

The fourth floor of the Moon River Brewing Company, the most haunted floor in the building. People have been physically attacked by unseen forces here for many years. *Photo by Ryan Reese*

There is an abundance of haunted locations throughout the Historic District of Savannah and the surrounding area, but few are as well known to the paranormal community as the Moon River Brewing Company, located at 21 West Bay Street. Employees, guests, and paranormal investigators alike have all witnessed the powerful entities that have haunted this building for many years. There have been numerous reports of witnesses being shoved, scratched, and attacked by unseen forces there. The paranormal activity occurs so often that even some of the world's most famous ghost hunting teams have investigated this very building. The SyFy Channel's television show *Ghost Hunters* filmed there with the The Atlantic Paranormal Society (T.A.P.S.) crew in 2005, and the Travel Channel's *Ghost Adventures* crew investigated in 2009. Both teams were able to catch some very compelling evidence of the hauntings occurring at the Moon River Brewing Company. Even still, paranormal activity occurs on an almost daily basis.

The Moon River Brewing Company, originally built as the City Hotel in 1821. *Photo by Ryan Dunn*

THE HISTORY

The current structure sits directly across the street from where Savannah's founder, James Edward Oglethorpe, pitched his tent and rested after the first day our colonists arrived in 1733. There was a prior structure located on the lot where Moon River Brewery now sits that was built, in 1809, for Robert and John Bolton. On January 11, 1820, a great fire burned almost everything from Bay Street to Broughton Street, this structure included. Nearly one year later, in the year 1821, a Charleston native named Eleazer Early purchased the empty lot and built the City Hotel, a grand hotel complete with beautiful, ornate architecture and a full downstairs bar. Savannah's elite would gamble and drink in the bar, as well as take rooms upstairs. The building also housed a post office and the Bank of the United States for a short period of time. What is now the Moon River Brewing Company currently resides in this very same building.

One evening, in August of 1832, two gentlemen got into an argument at the bar of the hotel. James Stark, a state legislator from nearby Glynn County, made a derogatory, racist remark about Dr. Philip Minis, an upstanding Jewish doctor in the community. Dr. Minis demanded that Stark make an apology, to which he vehemently refused. Minis then challenged Stark to a duel, but the two men could not come to an agreement as to the terms of the duel. A few nights later, on August 10, 1832, as James Stark was walking down the staircase from the third to the second floor of the hotel, Dr. Minis was walking up the same staircase. Minis proclaimed James Stark to be a coward, and Stark quickly reached into his breast pocket as if reaching for a gun. Dr. Minis retrieved his pistol first, and shot Stark directly in the chest. The bullet went straight through Stark's spine, killing him instantly.

To everyone's surprise, however, it turned out that James Stark was not even armed. Perhaps he drank too much that evening and possibly left his gun in his room, or maybe he was reaching for a cigar, a cigarette, or even a lighter—we will never know. In any case, Dr. Philip Minis was arrested for murder because he had shot and killed an unarmed man. After five months of incarceration, and a deliberating jury that took only two hours to decide his fate, Dr. Minis was miraculously acquitted of all charges.

The City Hotel continued to thrive for many years after the murder, and it underwent a complete renovation in the year 1851. A man named Peter Wiltberger had purchased the hotel, and he wanted the whole building remodeled. In order to draw attention to the newly renovated hotel, Wiltberger had a live lion and lioness on display in the basement. Surprisingly enough, no one was injured or maimed while the lions were in the hotel.

I found a disturbing article dating back to November of 1860 that appeared in the *New York Times* concerning Savannah's City Hotel. A New Yorker by the name of James Sinclair told his story to a *New York Times* reporter, who then published this story in the newspaper. Sinclair was on his way from New York to see his brother in Augusta, Georgia, and he had taken up temporary residence at Savannah's City Hotel along the way. Soon after arriving at the hotel, Sinclair was badgered with questions about his reasons for being in the city. The following day, he was asked by the city's "Vigilant Committee" to leave town. A few hours later, a man came up to Sinclair and asked to have a private word with him outside. He obliged, but as he stepped onto the sidewalk, he realized that he had walked into a trap. According to Sinclair, "Each man drew a revolver, and each man drew a bowie knife."

James Sinclair was then dragged through the city streets by the angry mob, all the way to Forsyth Park. He was kicked and prodded the whole way, as the crowd shouted obscenities due to the fact that he was a "New York Yankee." When they finally arrived at the park, Sinclair was ordered to undress, to which he ferverently refused. He was then forcibly undressed by the crowd until he was naked. The mob then ordered him to lie face down as he was lashed repeatedly with a cat o' nine tails, which caused lacerations and bruising. At the same time, the mob took turns rapping him on the head with the butt end of a pistol and kicking him in his ribs. After this torment went on for seemed to Sinclair like forever, he was then ordered to redress and was told that he would have a ten-second head start, before the crowd would start firing their pistols.

Sinclair quickly managed to leap over a fence and escaped the unruly mob. He then booked the first available passage out of the city on the steamship *Alabama*, which was bound for New York. After arriving back home, James Sinclair went straight to the *New York Times* office and relayed his story to a reporter.

The City Hotel closed its doors for good in 1864. General Sherman had arrived in Savannah with his Union troops in December of that year, and the hotel became a hospital during the War Between the States. There are also rumors that it was used as a makeshift hospital during the city's last Yellow Fever Epidemic in 1876. The property later went on to become a boarding house, a saloon, a storage warehouse, and later an office-supply company. In the year 2000, the building reopened its doors as the Moon River Brewing Company, Savannah's first craft beer brewery and restaurant.

RENOVATIONS

It wasn't long after opening its doors that the ghosts of the building decided to make themselves known. The restaurant wanted to expand its dining space and renovate the upper three floors of the building. Within the first couple of weeks, all of the contractor's men quit. They were complaining of extreme cold spots and of seeing apparitions pass through the halls. These men felt that the spirits of the brewing company were not at all happy about the renovations. The contractor, however, was not afraid of the ghosts, so he decided to finish the job himself. Everyday, his wife would meet him on the site and the two of them would have lunch together. One afternoon, as his wife was leaving, she was headed down the same staircase on which James Stark was murdered over 100 years earlier. As she started down the stairs, she felt a strong push from behind her, and she tumbled down the stairs. There was no one behind her and no way to explain the events that had just taken place. The contractor quit that afternoon and, to this day, the upper floors of the Moon River Brewing Company remain unfinished.

Oddly enough, however, the brewery became creative in 2012, and still managed to produce extra dining space. They purchased the empty lot next door to the brewery and turned it into a beer garden with plenty of extra seating. If you can imagine how much this lot cost, being at a prime location on the corner of Bay and Whitaker Streets, that should give you an idea as to how haunted the upper floors of this building are. They had to purchase a separate lot for extra dining space, when they have three perfectly good, unused floors already. When paranormal activity is influencing business decisions, you definitely have a serious case on your hands.

OTHER HAUNTINGS

Although the paranormal activity at the brewing company becomes more heightened during renovations, it still occurs on a regular basis. Members of the staff, patrons, and paranormal investigators alike have been pushed and scratched by unseen forces there. Although Savannah is one of the most haunted cities in the United States, this is one of the few locations where entities make physical contact on a regular basis.

There have even been reports of the apparition of a boy appearing in the basement, who the employees have nicknamed Toby. There are also accounts of a malevolent female apparition who haunts the third and fourth floors of the building. The staff has given her the name Mrs. Wilson, and they believe that she may be the one who causes harm to others. It is also believed that the ghost of James Stark may also haunt the place.

On more than one occasion, while closing up and being the last ones in the building, the staff has heard what sounds like a loud dance party going on in the basement. When they head downstairs, the noise suddenly stops. They have also heard loud footsteps racing back and forth above them on the upper floors, even though they are the only ones left in the building. Dark shadow figures have quickly passed by multiple staff members during the daytime and at night. Richard, one of the kitchen staff, recalls being violently pushed by an unseen force in the kitchen one morning as he was performing his opening duties. With all of this paranormal activity occurring at the Moon River Brewing Company, this place had been at the top of my list to investigate for quite a while. In August of 2011, I finally got my chance.

THE INVESTIGATION

I sat down in July with Brandi Cockram, the marketing director and events coordinator for the Moon River Brewing Company, to discuss the paranormal activity that they were experiencing in the building. As she told me about all of the encounters that occurred there, my eyes grew wide with excitement. I knew that I had stumbled onto a great location. Brandi continued to say that all of the investigators would be required to sign waivers in case any of us were hurt. I told her that we were used to this, since we tended to investigate abandoned buildings and dangerous areas. We had signed waivers before saying that if we were to get hurt or fall through a floor, the owners of the building would not be responsible.

"Well, that's part of the reason," said Brandi.

She then went on to tell me about how the spirits at the brewing company have attacked members of other paranormal investigation groups. Not long before, a female investigator from another team went to the third floor by herself during an investigation one night to conduct an EVP session. She came rushing down the stairs not five minutes later; both of her arms were covered in scratch marks and blood. She said that she had been violently attacked by a female apparition in a black dress. This is why we were required to sign waivers, just in case we were attacked by the entities in the building.

On another occasion, Brandi was opening the bar one morning after the restaurant had been investigated by a paranormal team the night before. Evidently, the team had stirred up the building's activity. Every time Brandi would go to make a drink for her customer that morning, a rocks glass would unexplainably shatter in her hands. A few attempts and many cuts later, she finally gave up. They had to close the restaurant that morning because the ghosts of the building were not being very cooperative. When we arrived on a dark and stormy night on August 12, 2011, to conduct our investigation, none of us knew what we were in for.

We arrived with a team of six of investigators, including myself, David, Sara, and Brandon Dahlin, and two other outside investigators. It doesn't happen very often, but every once in a while, we do allow others to join us on our investigations. On this particular night, we had Veronica Stephens from South Carolina, and Kevin Ford from Atlanta, Georgia, join us. We met downstairs at 10 p.m. as the restaurant was closing to discuss the details of the investigation and the layout and history of the building. We decided to split up into two teams, which would remain two floors apart at all times to avoid any cross-contamination of evidence.

As we walked from room to room getting initial readings, the air in the building became more and more dense. When we approached the third floor, the heavy, malevolent presence could easily be felt. On the fourth floor, the air was so thick you could cut it with a knife. There was this very intense feeling that something, or someone, did not want us up there. It was no surprise that Brandi had said the upper floors and the basement were the most haunted areas of the building. We were still conducting our initial readings and we were already feeling its presence.

EVPs

While walking through the basement with my team, Brandon asked: "Where's Veronica?" We then captured a chilling EVP of a male spirit that whispered: "Wish she was dead." A few hours later, in the same room, we caught the same spirit voice, but this time it whispered: "Get out, get out." Towards the end of the investigation, at 4:55 a.m., we captured yet another EVP in the basement, but this one was in a language that we did not recognize. It sounded as if the entity had shouted: "Nyoushka Bosha." We later had this clip analyzed, and it turns out that it is in the African Zulu language. It translates: "Get out. You will burn." This clip was captured in the same basement that was destroyed by fire in 1820. Could this be the spirit of an old slave that perhaps died in the fire warning us of impending doom? We may never know, but the clip itself does match the history of the building.

Although we managed to capture some very compelling evidence in the basement of the building, the fourth floor also proved to be extremely active. This was definitely the most uncomfortable area in the whole building. The dense, dismal feeling of the fourth floor was almost unbearable. As we conducted our EVP session there, the air seemed to get thicker by the minute. We soon caught a male spirit whispering: "Help me," directly into our digital recorder. This was captured near the back corner of the fourth floor by the old hotel's elevator shaft. I then asked: "Can you show yourself to us?" The same male spirit then answered: "No." I asked: "Are you trying to hide from us?" The same entity then replied: "I am."

OTHER EXPERIENCES

During an eight-hour investigation of the Moon River Brewing Company, we were able to capture multiple pieces of audio evidence. In addition, we had numerous personal experiences while there, and experienced many levels of paranormal activity. From uncomfortable feelings throughout the building, primarily the upper floors, to flashlights turning on and off by themselves, we knew for sure that the building was most definitely haunted. As we were packing up our equipment on the main floor, we had one last encounter with the ghosts of the brewery. Everyone in the building (six of us, plus one restaurant manager, who was required to stay with us that evening) was on the main floor packing up. All of a sudden, we heard numerous footsteps trampling loudly back and forth from above us. Evidently, we had stirred up the ghosts during our investigation. We quickly said our goodbyes and left. Eight hours in that building alone was more than enough time for us, and we had managed to capture some great paranormal evidence throughout the evening.

To this day, the Moon River Brewing Company continues to be a highly active paranormal hotspot in Savannah. It doesn't appear that the ghosts are ready to settle down any time soon.

On a lighter note, the brewery does make great beer! I recommend the Swamp Fox I.P.A. or the Apparition Ale, named after the spirits that continue to haunt the place. If you ask nicely, they may even let you walk through the basement and the second floor. The 3rd and 4th floors, however, are closed to the public, because they are unfinished and people do get attacked up there. Be sure to bring an audio recorder though—you never know what you may catch!

CHAPTER 10

The Haunted Inn
THE RIVER STREET INN
INVESTIGATION

The River Street Inn occupies an old cotton warehouse dating back to 1817. *Photo by Ryan Reese*

With beautiful, antique rooms fronting both Bay and River Streets, the River Street Inn is definitely one of the nicest stays in the city of Savannah. Before moving to this wonderful city in 2007, my wife and I stayed there for five nights on our honeymoon, and this is part of what sold us on Savannah. We moved to the city three years later and, to this day, it was one of the best decisions that we have ever made.

THE HISTORY

The inn itself is nestled in a fully restored cotton warehouse dating all the way back to the year 1817. All of the rooms are furnished with antique period pieces and the staff is top-notch. This may be one of the most beautiful inns in the city, but there is a darker side as well. Since it's reopening as an inn, in 1987, guests and employees have experienced all manner of paranormal activity throughout the building.

Although the bottom portion of the River Street Inn was built in 1817, the top three floors were not added until many years later, in 1853. The bottom two floors of the building were the original cotton warehouse where the slaves worked, the third floor was used for additional storage, and the fourth and fifth floors were used as offices for the cotton factors. Many of the slaves who lived in these warehouses did so under extremely harsh conditions. They were overworked throughout the day, and then they were not even afforded the comfort of a blanket at night. A blanket was considered to be a fire hazard, so many of them died from sickness, cold, and exposure to the elements in these buildings. One of the greatest fires to ever destroy Savannah began because of this very reason.

On January 11, 1820, a fire broke out in a livery stable near the river at around two o'clock in the morning. A slave had built a small fire to keep warm and the fire got out of hand. Over the next twelve hours, the city fought tirelessly against the raging flames. By the time the fire was finally extinguished, almost everything from River Street to Broughton Street had been destroyed. Savannah lost a total of 463 structures that day, which, in those days, was the majority of the city. The building that is now the River Street Inn was also destroyed by the fire.

The upper two floors of the River Street Inn were built with floor-to-ceiling windows to allow maximum light for the cotton factors as they worked. A cotton factor's job was to oversee the cotton being imported and exported from the warehouse, as well as to sell the cotton for the planters. They were able to look out of large office windows and watch the merchant cargo ships arriving and departing from the harbor of Savannah. The bottom floors of the warehouse were built with wide-arched doorways to allow for the easy transport of large bales of cotton from one area to another. The area of River Street where the inn now sits is known as Factor's Walk, named after the factors that would walk up and down these paths grading the cotton. There is a labyrinthine maze of alleys and walkways still there that were once used long ago to make the transporting of cotton easier.

The cotton warehouse that houses the old inn was originally built for George Wymberly Jones, the grandson of Noble Jones. Noble Jones is most noted for building the famous Wormsloe Plantation on the Isle of Hope, just outside of town, and the Jones family is one of the oldest founding families in the city. The structure remained in their hands until the late 1890s, when it then became a small grocery store. The building went on to become a ship chandlery, a boathouse, and then the home of the United States Coast Guard's Captain of the Port. In 1986, the structure underwent extensive renovations to become the River Street Inn. In 1998, the adjoining building was purchased, and the inn almost doubled in size from forty-four rooms to eighty-six rooms.

THE HAUNTS

In May of 2011, I was afforded the opportunity to sit down with Regina Graham, the Director for Sales and Marketing at the inn, to discuss the paranormal activity that they were experiencing there. According to her, there were four rooms in particular that seemed to be the most active. Rooms 303, 335, 518, and 526 have had more reports of strange phenomena than any of the other rooms in the inn, although guests and employees have had numerous experiences throughout other parts of the hotel as well.

FIFTH FLOOR

A couple staying on the fifth floor reported hearing the sounds of children's laughter in the halls, only to find no one present upon investigating. When they reported the incident to the desk clerk, he said that there were no children staying on the floor that particular evening. As they went back to their room, they felt a very heavy thickness in the hallway around their feet. They explained that it felt as if they were trudging through a thick mud, although there was nothing to be seen near their feet.

ROOM 518

There are numerous reports about the activity that happens in room 518, especially near the bathroom. Guests' items tend to get moved around by themselves there, only to reappear in the oddest of places. On more than one occasion, a guest has gotten out of the shower, only to find the cryptic words "We are here" written across the foggy bathroom mirror.

ROOM 303

In room 303, a man and woman reported hearing strange noises coming from their bathroom, as they lay in bed late one evening. It sounded as if someone were fumbling through their things, and the sounds of drawers and cabinets being opened and shut kept occurring in the room. They knew that there was no one else with them, because they had not yet fallen asleep, yet these strange sounds kept occurring throughout the night. The couple later fell asleep, only to both awaken in the middle of the night to witness a frightening sight. A female apparition in a long, gray dress was sitting on the end of the bed that they were in! As soon as it appeared, and they both saw it, the apparition suddenly vanished as quickly as it had come. The couple was astonished by what they had just witnessed only five feet away from them. The first thing in the morning they went downstairs and told the desk clerk what they had witnessed the night before. According to the clerk, this wasn't the only time that an apparition had appeared to a guest in this particular room.

ROOM 335

On another occasion, a housekeeper at the inn was making her daily rounds one summer afternoon, when she arrived at room 335. She opened the door and walked into the room to begin her usual cleaning routine. As she rounded the corner, she was horrified to see the apparition of a man lying in the bed before her. He seemed so real that she could even see the imprint of a person in the blankets, as if someone were lying in the bed, yet she could see right through this apparition. She screamed as loud as she could, and another housekeeper came rushing into the room. As they both looked at the bed, there was no one there.

According to the inn's reservation system, the room was listed as unoccupied. The housekeeper could not rationalize what she had just witnessed, and she quit her job at the inn the following day.

THE INVESTIGATION

After concluding my interview with Regina, I realized that we had to investigate this place! I had spent my honeymoon here, and now I was about to finally have the chance to investigate the old inn. We could not set a date until August 13, 2011, because the summer was their busy season, so I would be forced to wait patiently all summer. When the day finally arrived, I could not wait until that evening. I had all of our equipment charged and packed the night before, so I was ready to go as soon as my feet hit the floor that morning. The investigation didn't begin until midnight, however, so I had quite a few hours to kill. I spent the day milling about the Historic District, trying to keep my mind occupied until nightfall. When we finally arrived at the River Street Inn at around 11:45 that night, I could not wait to get inside.

EVPs

As we were collecting initial readings in room 335, our guest investigator that evening began to freak out. He was very distraught and kept saying that he didn't feel right in that particular room. A few seconds later, one of our audio recorders captured an EVP of a woman that mischievously whispered: "Make him scared." I strongly believe that this spirit we captured on recording was trying to antagonize this particular investigator. Later on, in that same room, we caught a male entity on a recording that whispered: "Come on."

Although we were getting some interesting results in room 335, it was room 303 that seemed to give off the most negative energy in the building. Paranormal activity seemed to radiate from that particular room.

All investigators present that night had the same mutual feeling about room 303. The air in the room was very dense, and there was the overall sense of dread permeating the air. There was also the overwhelming feeling of an unseen malevolent presence not wanting us there. Soon after, we were able to capture some compelling audio evidence to support our intuitions. As I was setting up the infrared light on one of our night vision video cameras, my digital recorder captured the voice of a male spirit who strongly whispered the word: "Kill."

Later on in the evening, our equipment started malfunctioning in this same room. Our cameras started to power down one by one, and one of our flashlights kept going on and off by itself. I then captured an EVP of the same male voice from earlier, but this time he growled: "Get out." After exiting the room, the equipment that had just malfunctioned in the room started working normally again.

SCRATCHED AND THE FIFTH FLOOR

As the evening progressed, we advanced to the fifth floor of the building. As we headed down the hallway, a tall, dark shadow figure quickly darted past us and then disappeared further down the corridor. We were all in shock from what we had just witnessed. You could easily make out the human shape of the apparition, but you could not make out any features. The creature was three dimensional, and it was the darkest color of black that you could ever imagine—and over six feet tall. Seconds later, three unexplained scratch marks suddenly appeared on one of our investigator's arms. The scratches were deep enough to draw blood. Could this shadow figure have done this as it passed by? We had just arrived at the fifth floor, and we were already having physical contact. We proceeded to investigate room 518, one of the most haunted rooms on this floor.

Within the first five minutes of being in room 518, we began to hear heavy footsteps pacing back and forth, and the sound was coming from up above us. We were on the top floor of the building, and there was no one walking on the roof at two o'clock in the morning, at least not anyone living. The sounds began to get louder and louder—much too loud to be rodents or any other animal. These were human footsteps, and they were not treading lightly. We did also manage to capture a few recordings in this room of some strange, unexplained whispering, but nothing significant enough to really make out what was actually being said.

As the sun began to come up that morning, we decided to wrap things up. We concluded our investigation of the River Street Inn and went home for some much-needed rest. We were thoroughly exhausted from our adventurous night and it was time for breakfast and a good long sleep. There was a ton of footage to go through and edit, and we had captured some great paranormal evidence throughout the night. We were very privileged to be the first paranormal investigation team to ever investigate the River Street Inn and, to this day, I don't think anyone else has ever had the opportunity. It still remains one of the most beautiful stays in all of Savannah, as well as one of the most haunted.

CHAPTER 11

Guests that Never Leave
THE 17HUNDRED90 INN
INVESTIGATION

The 17hundred90 Inn, home to one of the most famous ghost stories in Savannah. *Photo by Ryan Reese*

The 17hundred90 Inn and restaurant is home to one of Savannah's most famous ghost stories. Reported to be haunted by the ghost of a beautiful, young Irish girl named Anna, this inn is a huge destination spot for ghost hunters and paranormal enthusiasts around the world. I would like to start first by saying that the inn is indeed haunted, but for completely different reasons altogether from that which you may have heard. A lot of the inn's original history has been interwoven with folklore and urban legend, so I will separate fact from fiction, as I tell you the true tale of the 17hundred90 Inn.

THE HISTORY

There are many different variations of this tale, but it goes something like this: In the late 1700s, an Irish indentured servant named Anna Powers lived and worked in the home as a young girl. Years later, she fell in love with a young sailor who sailed away to Europe and never returned. (In other variations of the story, Anna was betrothed to marry a wicked, old miser who kept her locked away.) In either case, Anna fell into a deep depression and, eventually, took her own life by jumping out of the third-story window, straight to her death on the flagstones below.

This is one of the biggest ghost stories in Savannah, yet I can find no historical proof that a lady named Anna ever took her life by jumping from that window. There are no records of suicide at all throughout the home's extensive history. Even though Anna was a servant, there would have been some record of her death, or at least an article in the newspaper—something. I did find record of one Anne and two different Annas that lived in the home, but none of them died from jumping out a window.

The real history of the 17hundred90 Inn goes more like this: The home, located at the corner of Lincoln and East President Streets, which is currently the 17hundred90 Inn, was built in the year 1820 for Steele and Ann Matthews White. Although there are claims that the structure dates back to the year 1790 (hence the inn's name), tax assessments show that the home wasn't built until many years later, in 1820. I believe the reason they didn't name the place the 1820 Inn was because of all of the tragedies that befell Savannah in that year. The first major Yellow Fever Epidemic in Savannah occurred that year, as well as a great fire that destroyed much of the city. As I said, I can understand why they didn't name it the 1820 Inn, but as to why they picked the year 1790...I have no clue.

About six months before the house was completed, Steele White died at an early age, leaving young Anne a widow. Anne White continued to live in the home with her son, William P. White, and her daughter, Anna M. White, until she died of a "softening of the brain" in the home in, December of 1861. According to James Caskey, author of *Haunted Savannah* and owner of Cobblestone Ghost Tours, this "probably refers to a series of increasingly debilitating strokes, or an abscess." His determination is most likely the case. If you decide you would like to read even further into the tale of Steele and Ann White, Caskey covers their history with a keen eye to detail and truth in his 2013 edition of his book *Haunted Savannah*.

Her daughter, Anna M. White, married a man named Lewis J.B. Fairchild and lived there until the late 1800s. The only other name of Anna to come up in the history of the building is Anna M. Powers, who lived in the home from 1879 until the year 1934. This was the first and last incident of the name Anna as the woman who supposedly took her life by leaping from the third-story window, and the suicide story also doesn't add up. In 1934, Anna M. Powers died at the age of 93, and according to her death certificate, she died of Cardio Vascular Renal Disease.

Interestingly enough, she was born in Ireland and arrived in the states in the year 1853, but she was never an Irish indentured servant. By the time she moved into the home located where the 17hundred90 is now, it was 1879, which was years after slavery and indentured servitude. Unfortunately, none of these women match the story of Anna that we have come to know all too well.

73

CERTIFICATE OF DEATH
GEORGIA DEPARTMENT OF PUBLIC HEALTH
Bureau of Vital Statistics

1. PLACE OF DEATH

County **CHATHAM**

City or Town **SAVANNAH, GA.** Militia District (Number and Name) _____ Registered No. **1792**

Street and Number (No.) _____ (Street) **128 Lincoln St.** Mos. ____ Ds. ____ NON-RESIDENT (Yes or No) _____ State of Georgia

(If death occurred in a hospital, give its name instead of street and number) _____ Ward _____

2. FULL NAME **Mrs Anne M. Powers**

Residence (City or Town) **Savh. Ga.** (Street and Number)

PERSONAL AND STATISTICAL PARTICULARS

3. SEX **Female** 4. COLOR OR RACE **White** 5. Single, Married, Widowed, Divorced (write the word) **Widow**

6. DATE OF BIRTH (month, day, year) **Dec. 10, 1841**

7. AGE **93** Years | Months | Days | If less than one day Hours ____ Minutes ____

8. OCCUPATION
(a) Trade, profession or particular kind of work done, as spinner, sawyer, bookkeeper, etc.
(b) Industry or business in which work was done, as cotton mill, sawmill, bank, etc.
(c) Date deceased last worked at this occupation (month and year)
(d) Total years spent in this occupation

9. BIRTHPLACE (P. O. Address) **Ireland**

10. NAME **John Carrick**

11. BIRTHPLACE (P. O. Address) **Ireland**

12. MAIDEN NAME **Honora O'Hayer**

13. BIRTHPLACE (P. O. Address) **Ireland**

14. INFORMANT (Signed) **Miss L. Lille Powers**
(Address) **128 Lincoln St.**

19. BURIAL PLACE (Cemetery) **Cathedral Cem**
(Postoffice)

20. UNDERTAKER (Signed) **Albert Goette** Date **Dec. 27/34**
(Address) **123 Habersham**

MEDICAL CERTIFICATE OF DEATH

16. DATE OF DEATH **Dec. 26, 1934** 3 A/ (Month, Day, Year) ____ 19 ____ at ____ (Hour) ____ M

17. I HEREBY CERTIFY, That I attended the deceased from **12/25/34** 19 ____ to **18/26/34** 19 ____

I last saw h____ alive on **12/26/34** 19 ____, death is said to have occurred on the date and hour stated above.
The principal cause of death and related causes of importance in the order of onset and duration of each:

Cardio Vascular Renal Disease

Other contributory causes of importance:

Senility

What test confirmed diagnosis? (Specify whether autopsy, operation, laboratory, or clinical)

If death was due to external causes (violence) fill in also the following:
Was injury an accident, suicide, or homicide?
Where did injury occur (Specify city or town. If outside of limits, the county, and also the state)
Did injury occur in a home, public place or industry?
Manner of injury
Nature of injury

(Signed) **J. R. Broderick** M.D.
(Address) **415 Abercorn**

15. FILED **DEC 25 1934**

(Signed) **Eva L. Righton** 19 ____
(Local Registrar)

The death certificate of Anne Powers (Anna) who actually died of heart failure, not suicide.

In the 1900s, the building changed ownership multiple times, and we did find a few other natural deaths in the home. In 1979, it became the 17hundred90 Inn and restaurant, and remains so to this very day. The ghosts that haunt the 17hundred90 Inn are mainly attributed to the slave history of the building. In those days, the slaves were kept in the basement, which is now the restaurant and bar of the inn.

THE HAUNTINGS

There are the ghosts of at least two slaves that haunt this building still.

PENNIES AND DIMES

In the restaurant and bar area, there is the ghost of a six-year-old slave boy named Thaddeus. Guests and employees find stacks of pennies and dimes in the oddest locations. This strange phenomenon has occurred so frequently over the years, that the staff feels they are definitely paranormal occurrences. These coins have appeared between the bricks in the old basement, on tables, and many other places in random fashion. They just seem to appear out of thin air. Guests have even lost bracelets and rings, only to find them on the nightstand the next morning surrounded by a circle of pennies or dimes. This strange business has been attributed to the ghost of Thaddeus.

If you were a slave in those days, you were not allowed to own property, including coin. If you were found with money in your possession, even the smallest amount of change, you could be accused of theft or of trying to save money to buy your freedom. You would be severely punished, beaten, lose a hand, or even be executed for such a crime. If a slave ever found any change, they would hand it over to the first white person that they saw. We believe that this may be why Thaddeus leaves stacks of pennies and dimes everywhere.

Although the name suggests that the building was built in 1790, tax assessments show that the structure wasn't built until 1820. *Photo by Ryan Reese*

HATTIE

There is the ghost of yet another slave that haunts the downstairs as well, and the staff has given her the name "Hattie." She was said to be a "Geechee" slave, deeply involved with black magic and voodoo. Hattie haunts the kitchen on the first floor, and she is very possessive over her area. Members of the kitchen staff have been attacked by an unseen presence there on more than one occasion. Pots and pans have been unexplainably thrown across the room, and there have been reports of people being shoved by phantom hands. These paranormal occurrences in the kitchen have been blamed on Hattie, who is supposedly very protective of what she feels to be her kitchen.

MAKE A WISH

Although my wife and I do own our own ghost tour company called Afterlife Tours, our paranormal investigation team, the Savannah Ghost Research Society, is completely nonprofit. We do not charge for our investigations, and we constantly assist the citizens of Savannah with the hauntings in their homes. In July of 2011, I was approached by the Make a Wish Foundation to conduct a paranormal investigation here in Savannah. The boy's name was Cody, and his wish was to come to Savannah and go ghost hunting. He was from New York, and he had a keen interest in studying the paranormal. The foundation booked him room 204, also known as Anna's Room, at the 17hundred90 Inn. This was reported to be the most haunted room in the inn, haunted by the ghost of Anna herself. The Inn had our team come in to conduct a full, overnight paranormal investigation with Cody. I decided to go this one alone, with Cody and his mother, Tammy, investigating with me.

The week before the investigation, I met with Patrick Godley, the owner of the inn, to discuss the history and hauntings surrounding the building. We spoke for almost an hour, and he told me about the ghosts of Thaddeus, Hattie, and Anna, as well as a few others. Patrick and his family had just recently purchased the inn the year before, and yet he still had an abundance of ghost stories to tell about the place. Not only had he and his staff encountered the paranormal there, but his parents had as well.

Patrick's father, Nathan Godley, was closing up downstairs late one evening, and he was behind the main desk in the lobby area of the building. The cooks and wait staff had gone home some hours earlier, and all of the guests were upstairs in their rooms. All of a sudden, a very tall man wearing a long, dark coat walked past him down the hallway and into the bar. His father followed the man into the bar to tell him that they were closed—but there was no one there. All of the doors to the building had been locked earlier in the evening, so there would have been no place for this man to go—he had just disappeared into thin air.

In Anna's Room, guests have reported all manner of paranormal activity. Items left on the nightstand and dressers get moved around all the time in the middle of the night. Guests, especially females staying in this room, have reported being physically shoved out of bed during the night by phantom hands. There have even been reports of them having their feet tickled by unseen fingers. The sound of glass breaking occurs overnight on occasion, only to discover when investigated that nothing is out of place

A mannequin sits in the third-floor window from which Anna Powers supposedly jumped to her death many years ago. *Photo by Ryan Dunn*

or broken. Some like to argue that this is the sound of Anna leaping out of the window to her death, but if this room is indeed haunted by the ghost of Anna, it is not the same Anna that we have come to know throughout Savannah's folklore. This would have been a much older Anna at the time of her death, according to historical records, and she never jumped from a window—she died of old age.

After interviewing Patrick for quite awhile, I believed that the inn was haunted, but I was excited to find out its true history. Cody would be arriving in Savannah in less than a week, and I had a lot of work to do at the historical society in order to prepare for our upcoming investigation. I thanked Patrick for all of his help and for letting us do this investigation. He really knew his history about the building, and he was a great help in piecing everything together.

THE INVESTIGATION

On August 24, 2011, I investigated the notoriously haunted 17hundred90 Inn and restaurant with Cody and Tammy. We had dinner before the investigation at the Chart House, since it was also a great haunted location in town. I brought Cody a copy of our Chart House investigation case file, and told him about the experiences we had during our investigation there a few months before. We finished our dinner and arrived back at the inn at around 9:30 p.m. to begin our investigation.

EVPS AND PHOTO MISHAP

We headed straight for room 204 and began to unpack all of the equipment. Cody pulled out a Ouija board and explained to me that the inn kept it here in this room for their guests to use as they wish. No wonder this room was so haunted; there is no telling what that board had conjured up over the years. We did not use it in the investigation, however. I am a firm believer in Ouija boards, and I do believe that they work. I also believe that they can be very dangerous; we use only scientific equipment on an investigation to gather our data.

As with all investigations, the first thing I did was turn on my digital audio recorder. As I was setting up my full-spectrum video camera on the tripod, a male voice was captured on my audio recorder saying: "Hey." It seemed as if it was trying to get our attention, because less than a minute later, we captured the same voice saying the same thing. Three minutes after that, we caught the same voice yet again, but this time he said: "Hi." Something was definitely trying to make contact with us. Later on in the evening, we did capture a few voices that sounded like female moans and voices in the room, but they were too faint to make out exactly what was being said.

One of the most disturbing audio clips, however, was captured in the second floor hallway as we headed downstairs. As we descended, my audio recorder caught an EVP of a man that moaned: "Help me." He sounded as if he were in extreme pain and in bad need of help. As with most EVPs, I did not hear this clip until I arrived back home and started reviewing the evidence. Once we arrived in the restaurant, we captured even more evidence of the ghosts that haunt the 17hundred90.

As we walked through the dining rooms on the first floor, Cody began taking pictures with his digital camera. In one of the dining rooms, he decided to take a picture of the fireplace, but he wasn't able to. His camera, all of a sudden, started jamming up and making really odd mechanical sounds. He turned to the other side of the room and snapped a picture, and the camera worked fine. He returned his viewfinder to the fireplace, and the camera started to malfunction again. This occurred three or four times before Cody finally gave up. Whatever presence was in the room with us, it would not allow a picture to be taken by the fireplace. We later tried to debunk the phenomena and couldn't.

As we rounded the corner to the next dining room, I captured yet another EVP. This one whispered: "Hey, there's no place to hide." I believe that this entity may have been trying to hide from us, as we entered the room with our video cameras. We later caught a male entity on recording that whispered: "You've got us." I could not explain either of these two clips or the message that these spirits were trying to get across to us. I do know, however, that we were the only living people in the room, and that there was no rational explanation for what we were experiencing on location.

PERSONAL EXPERIENCES

We investigated the inn fairly late into the evening, and we had a few personal experiences as well. While standing near the piano, Cody felt something brush past his right arm. Along with the audio evidence, we were able to document some drastic, unexplainable temperature drops in Anna's room, as well as throughout other spots in

Cody and his mother, Tammy, enjoying Savannah at night.

the building. On numerous occasions, we experienced equipment problems, many of which we could not explain.

After a great night of investigating, it was time to finish things up. I had only two days to review and edit all of the evidence before Cody left town, and I wanted him to have a copy of everything before he returned to New York. Over the next few days, I was astonished at some of the evidence we had managed to capture.

The 17hundred90 Inn is indeed haunted, and crawling with ghosts, but not from the popular ghosts still shared in numerous stories throughout Savannah. If you don't believe me, you should go and stay there for yourself. There is a very good chance that you will have a personal encounter with one of their resident ghosts.

MAKE-A-WISH FOUNDATION

Cody still lives in New York, and is doing well.

To become a part of the Make-A-Wish Foundation, or to donate or refer a child, please visit www.wish.org. The Make-A-Wish Foundation on average grants one wish every 38 minutes to a child with a life-threatening medical condition in the United States and surrounding territories.

CHAPTER 12

Exit Stage Left
THE SAVANNAH THEATRE INVESTIGATION

THE HISTORY

For nearly 200 years, the historic Savannah Theatre has graced the east end of Chippewa Square. Built in 1818 by renowned Savannah architect William Jay, the Savannah Theatre is the second oldest continuously operating theatre in the United States of America. The only theater that is older is the Walnut Street Theatre in Philadelphia, Pennsylvania, which dates back to 1809. William Jay is also well known for his work in designing the Owens-Thomas House, the Telfair Museum, and the William Scarbrough House in Savannah. Over the years, many famous performers have graced the stage of this theatre, including the likes of Oscar Wilde, W.C. Fields, John Wilkes Booth and his brother Edwin Booth, the Three Stooges, Lionel Barrymore, and Sarah Bernhardt—just to name a few.

Even as far back as 1895, there is evidence of the hauntings at the old theatre. On May 5th of that year, an article concerning the ghosts of the theatre appeared in the *Savannah Morning News*. The reporter for the newspaper interviewed the theatre manager, Tomlinson Fort Johnson, who had some interesting things to say about the ghosts that haunt the place. According to Mr. Johnson, on several occasions, chorus girls have run out of the dressing room and into McDonough Street "in a body, and in all the varied states of undress, trembling with fright over some imaginary evil that threatened them." In addition, policemen making rounds through Chippewa Square in the wee hours of the morning, in the late 1800s, reported hearing thunderous applause coming from the theatre, although it had been closed for hours.

The theatre that exists today, however, is not William Jay's original 1818 design. Tragically, the theatre has burned to the ground due to fire on two separate occasions, and the only thing remaining from 1818 is the original backstage wall of the theatre. They were able to salvage the wall and rebuild the theatre around it on both occasions, but the rest of the building had to be entirely redone. The first fire occurred on the evening of September 21, 1906. The theatre was going to feature Thomas Dixon's controversial play *The Clansmen*, and the building caught fire before the show began. It was suspected as arson, and a young actress, who was only eighteen years old, died in the fire. In those days, the dressing room of the theatre was under the stage to conserve space, and when the fire erupted, she was trapped underneath. The original structure was made of wood, so the building was engulfed in flames rather quickly. The walls of the theatre collapsed and the actress was burned alive. Despite the Klan's best efforts to halt the performance, the play was later shown in nearby Thunderbolt. There, members of the

Ku Klux Klan antagonized patrons as they entered the theatre in an effort to dissuade them from seeing the play.

Many years later, in 1931, the theatre was purchased by a man named Fred G. Weis, a motion picture magnate, who then turned the structure into a motion picture house. With the new era of motion pictures, plays weren't as popular anymore, and Mr. Weis opened a string of movie theatres throughout the city, including the Lucas and the Trustees Theaters. Not long after the theatre had reopened its doors, a second death occurred in the building. Patrons were watching a film one evening, when the second reel didn't come on. The house manager went upstairs to the projection booth to check on George, who was the projectionist working that evening. He assumed that maybe George had gone to the restroom or had possibly fallen asleep. As he entered the projection booth, he was shocked to find George lying there dead, slumped over the projector. He rushed over to George's body, but it was too late. George, who was in his mid-sixties, had unexpectedly passed away from a heart attack.

In 1948, the theatre caught fire yet again. This time, an eight-year-old boy named Benjamin tragically perished in the fire. He was with his parents in the balcony watching a movie one evening when the fire suddenly erupted. As everyone rushed out of the side exit door of the balcony to avoid the flames, Benjamin was trampled to death by the frightened mob of people. As the theatre walls collapsed from the engulfing flames, what was left of him burned in the fire.

Fred Weis had the theatre rebuilt once again, this time in its current Art Deco style. It wasn't until many years later, however, in 1981, that the theatre started showing plays once again. In 2002, it was sold to the Meece family from Branson, Missouri, who still own the place to this day. They are well known among locals and visitors for their musical revues and high-energy performances, as well as their resident ghosts. With all of the activity surrounding the Savannah Theatre, our team, the 3-D Ghost Hunters, had been trying to get into this location to investigate for quite a while.

In the fall of 2011, I received an unexpected, yet very welcome, phone call from Frank Sulkowski, the assistant news director and sports anchor for WJCL *ABC News* and WTGS *FOX News 28* in Savannah. The news stations wanted to do a story about the haunted locations of Savannah and its many ghosts, and Frank was going to be putting the story together himself. He asked if he could join us on an investigation to get the full experience for the story, and I readily agreed. There was just one problem; we didn't have any upcoming investigations booked for at least another month. We were still reviewing evidence from two prior investigations, but Frank wanted to film the following weekend. I was in a dilemma and had to come up with a solution very quickly.

At the time I was bartending at Ruth's Chris Steakhouse on Bay Street and ghost hunting as much as time would allow. That Saturday night, local jazz pianist and composer Eddie Wilson was performing at the restaurant. Later that evening, when he took a break, Eddie and I were talking and I spoke to him about my dilemma. "I can get you into the Savannah Theatre, and it's definitely haunted; I used to work there," said Eddie. He told me about how he had been the music director at the theatre for years, and he knew just who to call. I expressed my gratitude, and he agreed to call Dru Jones, the theatre manager, the following day. Dru had worked at the theatre for over ten years,

The Savannah Theatre at night. *Photo by Ryan Dunn*

and she had experienced paranormal encounters there on numerous occasions. After speaking with Eddie, she agreed to meet with me the following week for an interview, and to let us come in and film an overnight investigation with Frank and the news station.

As we followed Dru throughout the theatre during our initial walkthrough and interview, it didn't take long to realize that we had just hit the mother lode of haunted locations in Savannah. There were more ghost stories surrounding this particular building than there were for most of the other places that we had already investigated. For over 100 years, employees and patrons had reported experiencing all manner of paranormal activity, including apparitions, shadow figures, strange voices, and phantom footsteps—just to name a few. I couldn't wait to get back into the theatre at night with all of our equipment and conduct a full paranormal investigation of the place, and the weekend was only a few days away.

According to Dru, audience members had reported seeing a female in a white, lace dress disappear into the stage left exit door. This has happened on more than one occasion, and the patrons often mistook the apparition for part of the show. One evening during a show, Dru had been walking up the aisle to "grab a victim" from the audience to participate in the show. This part of the show was usually a nightly occurrence, but this evening was different. As Dru made her way up the aisle, she saw a female entity standing in the middle of the aisle blocking her way. She froze with fright, but then realized that she must continue the show, regardless of what she had just witnessed. As she attempted to regain her composure, she continued slowly up the aisle, and the apparition suddenly disappeared. Dru and the staff believe this to be the ghost of the young actress who died in the fire of 1906.

There have been many reports of activity in the balcony where the young boy named Benjamin died as well. On occasion, Dru runs the spotlight in the balcony during the show. There has been many times where she has felt what seems to be a small child tugging at the bottom of her shirt to get her attention. When she would turn around, all of the audience members were still in their seats, and there would be no one behind her. Many employees have also seen a small, dark, shadowy figure dart across the balcony toward the upper exit door. This very well may be the ghost of Benjamin trying to escape from the fire that once burned the theatre to the ground in 1948.

One evening, at around 2:30 in the morning, Dru and another female director were closing up and they were the last two people in the building. As they were turning out lights, the director accidentally turned on the house lights while the two of them were in the balcony dressing room, which used to be the projection booth where George died. All of a sudden, both women heard a deep man's voice shout: "What are you doing?" from right behind them. Frightened by what they heard, the two left the building in a hurry. The following night, at around the same time, they heard the voice again. Could this have been the ghost of George still haunting the theatre? I couldn't wait to find out. I thanked Dru for all of her help, and we agreed to meet for the investigation the upcoming weekend at the theatre at around 10:30 p.m.

The historic Savannah Theatre, the second oldest continuously operating theatre in America.
Photo by Ryan Dunn

THE INVESTIGATION

When we arrived at the theatre that evening, Biff Flowers, who worked for the news station, was already there setting up his camera. I introduced myself and my team, and we proceeded to unpack and get our base readings of electromagnetic fields, temperature, and humidity. Frank arrived shortly after, and we began our investigation. It wasn't long before the activity in the building started up and we captured our first two pieces of paranormal evidence, while still getting our initial base readings. As Kim was setting up a full-spectrum video camera on a tripod in the balcony area of the theatre, her digital voice recorder captured an EVP of a small boy saying: "Help me." This was in the same balcony where Benjamin was trampled to death over fifty years before. At around the same time, a static recorder in the lobby caught an EVP of a female spirit singing for over ten seconds. This could possibly have been the young actress who died in the fire in 1906. We had not yet finished setting up for the investigation and we were already capturing EVPs!

Later in the evening after the investigation had begun, I was in the old projection booth conducting an EVP session, when my audio recorder captured the voice of a male entity whisper "My Projector." I was standing in the very same spot where George had collapsed from a heart attack in the 1930's! We were early into the night and we were already catching compelling evidence that matched the deaths in the building. Later on, however, we caught one of the best pieces of video evidence that we have ever captured since becoming paranormal investigators.

Because we had heard the stories of the female apparition disappearing into the stage left exit door, we decided to set up a full-spectrum video camera facing the door, in an attempt to capture the spirit on video. While we were in the hallway of the main theatre conducting an EVP session, the video camera captured a white apparition of what appeared to be a head peek around the right side of the door frame and then disappear while still in the doorway. I believe that we managed to capture the young actress that died here in 1906 on video.

After we concluded our investigation of the historic Savannah Theatre, Frank showed our footage in a three-part series that aired on *Fox* and *ABC News* over a period of three consecutive nights. Thanks to Frank's high production quality and editing, this episode was later nominated for an Emmy and also won an AR Award. After all of the paranormal evidence that we managed to capture, Frank and the guys at the news station decided to give us our own local television series that they entitled *Spooky Town*. We have gone on to film with them at some of Savannah's most haunted locations, including the Foley House Inn, the Pirate's House Restaurant, and Fort McAllister in Richmond Hill.

A little over six months after our investigation of the Savannah Theatre, in the summer of 2012, I was contacted by the producers of A&E Biography's hit television show *My Ghost Story: Caught on Camera*. They wanted to see some of our best paranormal evidence, so I sent them our case file from the Savannah Theatre investigation. In July of that year, they flew Dru Jones and me out to Los Angeles to film on their set and then, a few weeks later, we met at the Savannah Theatre with their cameraman to shoot the B-roll footage here in town. The show finally aired on December 21, 2012, on Season 4 Episode 26, and it was part of a three-story episode entitled "Love Never Dies."

I owe a huge debt of gratitude to Eddie Wilson for introducing me to Dru Jones, who remains a dear friend to this day. If it weren't for Eddie, we might not have ever had the opportunity to investigate the historic Savannah Theatre at all. The spirits have not quieted down much and, often enough, employees and audience members alike experience the paranormal activity that occurs on a regular basis. I highly recommend seeing a performance there; it is one of the best shows in town. Dru still manages the old theatre, so stop by and introduce yourself if you see a show; she is one of the nicest people you will ever meet, and she also has a great sense of humor. Maybe that's how she has managed to work there for so long without being affected by the ghosts of the building. As they say, "the show must go on" and, at the Savannah Theatre, it has for nearly 200 years and hopefully will continue for many more years to come.

CHAPTER 13

War Cries
THE FORT MᶜALLISTER
INVESTIGATION

Fully restored by automobile mogul Henry Ford, the historic Fort McAllister is now a state park.
Photo by Ryan Dunn

THE HISTORY

Just about thirty minutes south of Savannah's famed Historic District, directly off of Interstate 95, lies Fort McAllister Historic State Park. The old fort is located in Richmond Hill, Georgia, which owes much of its town's development to none other than automobile mogul Henry Ford. Ford, who owned a winter home in the area, not only developed much of the city, but also oversaw the full restoration of Fort McAllister. The earthen redoubt fort sits on a bluff facing the Ogeechee River known as Genesis Point. Although the fort itself wasn't constructed until the year 1861, for use during the Civil War, the history of the land dates back some 350 years earlier.

The land at Genesis Point where Fort McAllister now sits used to be known as Guale, and it was once inhabited by the Spanish. Their mission of San Diego de Satuache was formerly located on or near this land. The Spaniards used Catholic missions such as this one to attempt to convert the local Creek Indians. By the end of the 1600s, the Spanish no longer inhabited the area. It wasn't until the mid-1730s, however, that English settlers arrived from Europe and started farming the land. In the mid-1800s, Lieutenant Colonel Joseph Longworth McAllister's family purchased Strathy Hall, a large plantation that also included the land at Genesis Point. When construction began on the fort in 1861, it was named after the McAllister family since the fort was on their land.

Fort McAllister, lost to Union troops on December 13, 1864. *Photo by Ryan Dunn*

The fort was an earthen structure constructed out of bricks made of sod and mud harvested by slaves from the nearby Ogeechee River. There were seven gun emplacements around its walls, and it was fully equipped with a hospital and a bunker for housing troops. The fort also housed a very impressive 10-inch mortar battery that had to be placed away from the walls of the fort because every time that it was fired, it would crumble the fort's earthen walls. In addition, there was a "Red Hot Shot" Furnace for the heating of cannonballs during times of attack. This "hot shot" was placed into a cannon and then fired at wooden ships, which would suddenly cause them to be engulfed in flames. Over the years, the fort and its 230 soldiers stationed there held off six separate attacks by Union troops that took place from July of 1862 until December of 1864.

The very first attack on Fort McAllister took place on July 1, 1862. Union ships had pursued the Confederate blockade runner, the *Nashville*, down the Ogeechee River all the way to the fort. Reports mentioned that the fort's earthen walls appeared to "swallow up"

This is a replica of the cannon that Confederate Major John Gallie was commanding when he was mortally wounded by enemy fire on February 1, 1863. *Photo by Ryan Dunn*

the cannon balls that were fired at it. After a few hours, the Union Navy finally gave up and retreated. Although there were no major casualties, this was the first minor victory for the small fort sitting on the bluff. It wasn't until about six months later, on January 27, 1863, that Union forces returned once again to try and take Fort McAllister. This time, they had brought their pride and joy, the famed ironclad ship the USS *Montauk*, which was equipped with a revolving turret and 11-inch and 15-inch smooth-bore cannons. Accompanied by a small fleet of wooden war ships, the Union Navy reportedly fired over 450 cannonballs at the fort, leaving large breaks in its earthen walls. Even with this impressive armada, the Union Navy was not able to take down the fort.

The following year, on February 1, 1863, the USS *Montauk* returned early in the morning, at around 7:45 a.m., to exact its revenge on Fort McAllister and finally overcome the Confederates. Although they failed in their attempt of capturing the fort, they did manage to kill one of the commanding officers. Confederate soldier Major John Gallie was mortally wounded in the battle as he was commanding one of the fort's 8-inch artillery positions. As gunfire bore down on the fort, a 15-inch Union shell ricocheted off of the cannon and decapitated the Major, exposing his brains. This was the only death during this battle, and although it was a Confederate victory, it was bittersweet nonetheless. Attacks were made once again on the fort, in February and March of 1863, but, as before, the fort held strong.

On March 3, 1863, during the fifth attack on the structure, the second Confederate casualty occurred. This time, the fort's mascot, a cat, was mortally wounded by cannon fire. The cat had arrived at the fort as a stray, and the troops adopted him as a mascot. For lack of a better name, they called him "Tomcat." Tomcat would strut back and forth across the battlements during battles, impervious to enemy fire. On this day, however, his luck had finally run out. He was buried as a soldier and listed as a confederate casualty of the war. Five days later, one more attack on Fort McAllister was made by Union ships, but to no avail.

On December 13, 1864, General William Sherman, accompanied by 4,000 union soldiers, descended on the fort of less than 300 Confederate troops. In an absurdly outnumbered battle that took less than 20 minutes, the Confederate fort fell to the hands of the North. Although they were at a very unfair disadvantage, it was reported that all of the troops stationed at Fort McAllister were either captured or died in battle. Never at any time did they ever surrender the fort. There were a total of 205 casualties altogether from the battle.

Fast forward to February of 2012, when I received a phone call from Frank Sulkowski of WTGS *FOX News 28* and WJCL *ABC News*.

"It's about time to film another *Spooky Town*," said Frank, as I answered the phone. "Do you have any ideas on a good location?"

I told him that I would get back to him later in the week, but that I did have a few ideas in mind. The week before, my next door neighbor and good friend Alan Gallardo had introduced me to photographer Ryan Reese. Reese used to work at Fort McAllister when he was in high school, and he was interested in seeing what our team might catch, should we be afforded a chance to investigate there. After I got off the phone with Frank, I gave Reese a call and asked if he could gain access to the fort for a night. He told me that although it had been a few years, he still knew the park manager, Daniel Brown, very well and he agreed to give him a call.

GROUND PATROL

Although Daniel Brown was a big skeptic when it came to the paranormal, he still agreed to let us conduct our overnight investigation, and he gave us full access to the fort. Daniel, though not a believer in ghosts himself, knew of multiple reports from others who had experienced encounters with the paranormal on the grounds of Fort McAllister over the years. In the 1960s, a groundskeeper was making his nightly rounds one evening when he suddenly encountered one of the entities that haunt the place. The apparition of a headless Confederate soldier walked right past him and then disappeared as quickly as it had come. The groundskeeper was right near the cannon where Major John Gallie was decapitated almost 100 years earlier in 1863, and this very well may have been the ghost of the major, still patrolling the grounds many years after his death.

HOSPITAL APPARITIONS AND MORE

More recently, a lady who was visiting Fort McAllister one afternoon witnessed the apparition of a Confederate soldier in the hospital bunker. As she rounded the corner, the woman was shocked to see the soldier lying in one of the bunk beds in the hospital. She ran out of the bunker in shock and quickly told the park managers about what she had witnessed. Other visitors have reported seeing apparitions of both Union and Confederate soldiers throughout the park's grounds over the years.

After interviewing Daniel, we decided that this would be the perfect location to film our second episode of our series *Spooky Town*. We set a date for the following weekend, and agreed to meet Frank and his cameraman, Biff Flowers, at midnight at the old fort on the night of the investigation.

THE INVESTIGATION

Before we left that afternoon, Ryan Reese and I decided to take a walk through the entire fort, bunkers and all. I wanted to get a feel for the place and decide where we would set up our video cameras during the night of the investigation. Reese used to work at the old fort, and he pointed out many tidbits of the fort's tragic history as we walked along. I turned on my digital voice recorder as we walked through the hospital bunker, because I was hoping to possibly catch some audio evidence. It turned out to be a good decision, because about five minutes into the recording, we captured a very clear EVP of what we think is a male soldier in the hospital barracks. As we rounded the corner, a man's voice was heard on the recording shouting: "Someone's standing on the roof!" Could this possibly be a residual EVP of a soldier warning of Sherman's attack on the fort in 1864? I wasn't sure, but we couldn't wait to get back to conduct a full overnight investigation.

As we drove down the long and winding road that led to Fort McAllister the evening of the investigation, we quickly realized that we were leaving civilization behind. The night itself was quiet and still, and the only sounds in the air were the songs of chirping crickets serenading the night. I had arrived that evening with Kim, Brandon and David Dahlin, Ryan Reese, and good friend Alan Gallardo, along with his girlfriend, Rose Gillespie. As we walked out to the fort that stands along the Ogeechee River with our equipment in tow, we met up with Biff, who was already beginning to set up. He informed us that Frank had just finished filming the late news that evening and that he was on his way there.

All of us had an uneasy feeling about the place, as did Frank when he arrived. It was easy to picture the fort as it would have been during the War Between the States, as it was set apart from the rest of the world and surrounded by woods. Aside from the gift shop and welcome center of the historic site, this place was isolated and preserved from the civilization of modern man.

EMF AND EVP READINGS

As we began our initial readings of the building, we quickly came to the realization that there were no areas in the fort that would give us a false EMF reading. The only power to the whole earthen fort was two strands of 75-watt light bulbs in the Hospital Bunker and the Powder Magazine. The wattage of these sources was so low that it did not even elicit a spike on our EMF detectors. This meant that if we were to later capture EMF spikes during our investigation, then we could very well document them as paranormal activity. It wasn't long into our investigation that we started experiencing high electromagnetic activity that we simply could not debunk. In the old hospital of the fort, we were receiving EMF readings of 20+ milligauss, which is fairly high, considering there was no power source to attribute the anomalous readings to.

During an EVP session in the hospital, Kim Dunn, our EVP Specialist, asked: "Can you make our EMF detector light up one more time to show us that you are here?" A male entity was then captured on an audio recorder angrily responding: "Get out."

Throughout the night, we managed to capture many other pieces of audio evidence that we could not explain. As we were walking outside the fort, near the old museum, my audio recorder caught an extremely clear EVP of a male spirit warning: "There's death if you want to move." We believe this could quite possibly be a residual entity of a field commander warning his soldiers to stay put. One of the most compelling pieces of evidence, however, was captured by Ryan Reese and Alan Gallardo in the Hot Shot Furnace of the fort. The two of them were conducting an EVP session in the furnace, and Reese had a flashlight in his hand. To try and get a reaction, Alan asked, "Can you make this flashlight turn off by itself?" A male spirit angrily responded: "I don't play games." Evidently the spirit haunting the furnace area of the fort was not in a playful mood.

Although we experienced anomalies in the Hot Shot Furnace as well as the Powder Magazine, the Hospital Bunker proved to be the most active area in regards to paranormal occurrences. In the early morning hours at around 3 a.m., the team was conducting an EVP session in the hallway of the old hospital. EMF readings were rising so high that they were off the charts, and there was an overall uneasy feeling throughout the bunker. All of a sudden, Frank felt a chilly, unseen presence pass directly through his body, as he stood against the wall in the hospital hallway. He described the feeling as being very cold and intense, and as creating a disturbing sense of dread. Later in the evening, Brandon heard phantom footsteps running up behind him in the same hallway, although he was completely alone in the bunker.

After spending many hours investigating Fort McAllister, we finally decided to call it a night. Between Biff's camera work, our recorders, and our video cameras, we had a ton of evidence to go through, and Frank wanted to try and air the show in a few days.

As we drove back down the dark, winding road leading away from the old fort, it was hard to shake the events of that night's investigation. We had definitely captured proof of the ghosts that haunt the historic Fort McAllister, and some of us had also experienced a few personal accounts that could not be explained. This location still proves to be one of the most haunted forts in the Savannah area, as well as a great lesson in history. Not only did we get great evidence of the paranormal here, but Ryan Reese became the newest member of the 3-D Ghost Hunters after the Fort McAllister investigation. He is still the team's photographer, as well as an active investigator in our group.

CHAPTER 14

Faces in the Mirror
THE SAVANNAH
HARLEY-DAVIDSON SHOP ON
RIVER STREET INVESTIGATION

Employees at the Savannah Harley-Davidson Shop on River Street have experienced all manner of paranormal activity, primarily on the second floor. *Photo by Ryan Reese*

Although I have had the opportunity to investigate many haunted locations all over the city of Savannah throughout the years, the investigations conducted on and around the River Street area tend to offer some of the most compelling pieces of paranormal evidence that my team has ever captured. When we were allowed overnight access to the Savannah Harley Davidson Shop on River Street, we were all excited. This was to be our fourth investigation location on River Street, so we were very familiar with all of the haunted history surrounding the area.

THE HISTORY

River Street is the oldest section of Savannah, and it is also the site of great suffering and sorrow. For many years, slaves were forced to live and work under horrible conditions in cramped cotton warehouses that lined the riverfront. There were deaths too numerous to count over the years as a result of these harsh conditions. The building that houses the Savannah Harley-Davidson Shop is just one of many of these cotton warehouses. As with the other warehouses, slaves were forced to work hard labor during the day and they slept in tight quarters upstairs on the second floor at night. If these walls could talk, they would speak of the human suffering that occurred in this building over the many decades of its existence.

This particular warehouse was originally built for a man named George Kollock and his wife, in the year 1854. The Kollocks resided there, and ran their family business from the building for many years, until George passed away in the home in 1889. Throughout the 1890s and early 1900s, the building was the site of the Standard Oil Company, and then it was once again converted into a warehouse. In the 1940s, the structure became the Atlantic Towing Company and Dock, and then it was used as the Ships of the Sea Museum from the 1970s to the late 1990s. When the Ships of the Sea Museum moved into the William Scarbrough house in 1996, Savannah Harley-Davidson acquired the property. It wasn't long after moving into the building that people began to experience all manner of paranormal activity.

UNEASY FEELINGS

Customers and employees started reporting uneasy feelings upon entering the building. Also, the sensation of being extremely dizzy and disoriented, as well as the feeling of being watched by unseen eyes has been reported. After conducting our investigation, we realized that these uneasy feelings could easily be explained by a natural reason. As we were doing our initial readings of the building, we documented very high electromagnetic fields (EMF) throughout the entire building. These high EMF readings were caused by multiple panel boxes and wiring throughout the store. High natural EMF fields have been known to cause uneasy feelings, as well as mild hallucinations in some cases. This could very well be the cause of these phenomena, but some of the other activities that the Harley-Davidson shop personnel were experiencing could not be explained quite as easily.

OTHER EXPERIENCES

Aside from the uneasy feelings experienced there, many have reported ice-cold temperature drops throughout the upstairs of the building, especially in the area near the bathroom.

Liz Kem, a salesperson at the shop, has had her own share of paranormal occurrences since she started working there. One fall afternoon, she was sitting behind the register downstairs working, and she was the only person in the building. All of a sudden, she heard the distinct sound of metal coat hangers sliding across the shirt racks coming from upstairs. It was almost as if someone—or something—was looking through the clothes. The sound kept occurring, and it seemed to be getting louder. As she slowly climbed the stairs to investigate the sound, the noise suddenly stopped. As she returned to the register downstairs, however, the noise started up again. After a few minutes, the sound subsided, but, for Liz, the day's end couldn't come soon enough.

Although some paranormal activity occurs downstairs, the upstairs of the shop tends to be the most active area of the building. Many customers have witnessed the apparition of a young female in a beautiful, lace gown pacing back and forth across the floors there. Others have witnessed a male figure, dressed in a suit and wide-brimmed hat, pass through the walls upstairs. Also, apparitions have been captured in photos by customers, while taking pictures in the floor-length mirror at the top of the stairway. Many times, the pictures would reveal a white, wispy apparition standing beside them in the mirror.

In 2011, a year before we had the chance to investigate the shop, a psychic who visited the building swore up and down that there was a portal to the spirit world just behind the bathroom wall upstairs. This is also where the toilet has been known to flush on its own accord on many an occasion.

One of the most disturbing occurrences in the building, however, involves the phantom voices of small children's laughter haunting the upstairs.

Salesperson Frances Sein has also had her share of experiences at the shop over the years. One afternoon, as she was working behind the counter downstairs, she heard a strange vibration sound coming from only a few feet above her. As she looked up, a wire sculpture of a motorcycle rider that hangs on the wall was rattling back and forth by itself. Even more unexplainable, however, was the thick wire hair on the sculpture waving listlessly, as if the hair were somehow blowing in the wind. The wire on this sculpture is so thick that it would take tremendous force just to make it budge, much less wiggle back and forth as effortlessly as it did.

THE INVESTIGATION

After hearing about all of the activity surrounding the old Harley-Davidson Shop, I decided to give them a call to see if they would be interested in having us come out to conduct an investigation. The following day, Frances returned my call and agreed to meet with me later in the week so that we could discuss the details. After interviewing Frances and Liz, we set up an investigation date for February 18, 2012, the evening after our Fort McAllister investigation. With two great locations lined up for the same weekend, I could barely contain my excitement for another two weeks.

HIGH EMF READINGS

When the day finally arrived to investigate the shop, we were all pumped up, but also a bit tired from the previous night's investigation and filming. I arrived that evening with investigators Kim, and Brandon and David Dahlin. Once we began to unpack and perform our initial readings, I was suddenly overcome with a strange dizziness. As we ascended the stairs, the feeling became much stronger. The air was very dense, and we all felt that we were not alone in the building. The area near the upstairs bathroom felt the most uncomfortable, and this was where we were getting the highest EMF readings. The high natural EMF levels throughout the store most definitely contributed to the uneasiness felt by all, but there was something else there too—something much more dark and sinister.

EVPs

As the investigation continued on into the night, the activity seemed to slowly escalate. Although it began with uneasy feelings and unexplained dizziness, it didn't stop there. As we were seated upstairs during an EVP session, we suddenly heard the unmistakable sound of metal coat hangers sliding back and forth across the racks by themselves. A few minutes later, an audio recorder, placed at the top of the stairs, captured a chilling EVP. A male spirit clearly whispered the name "George" into the recorder. Could this be the voice of George Kollock, for whom the home was originally built in 1854? He did die in the home years later.

Later in the evening, we managed to catch another chilling EVP, and this time it was right outside the bathroom door upstairs. An entity clearly says: "They got the girl" into an audio recorder. At about the same time, Liz, who had accompanied us on the investigation, felt as if she were being pulled by the arms, yet there was nothing around to rationalize this pulling sensation. As the night went on, more strange things began to occur. A little later, our EVP Specialist, Kim Dunn, caught a strong whiff of ladies' perfume near the downstairs register. The scent was unmistakable, and there was no one else on that floor with her at that time, since we were all still upstairs.

Throughout the entire evening, we had all experienced personal encounters with the paranormal. After returning home and reviewing hours-upon-hours of footage, we were able to compile more than enough evidence to deem the Savannah Harley-Davidson Shop on River Street to be extremely haunted. Although most of the activity centered around the second floor, there was a high level of electromagnetic energy throughout the entire building. This natural electromagnetic energy could be caused by too much wiring, panel boxes, or other power sources. Spirits, however, are drawn to this energy and use it to manifest themselves. The fact that there is a natural abundance of this energy in the building could be causing spirits to become attracted to the place.

Nonetheless, the paranormal activity at the old Harley shop still manages to occur on a regular basis. There is not a week that goes by without a customer reporting to an employee about their brush with the spirit world while visiting the place. Unexplained noises are still heard at closing, the upstairs toilet continues to flush by itself, and hangers can still be heard sliding across the clothes racks upstairs when no one else is in the building. With all of the unexplained phenomena that still occurs here, it may be quite a long time before the spirits finally decide to quiet down for good. Although it may be somewhat lesser known for its ghosts, this very well may be one of the most haunted locations on all of River Street.

CHAPTER 15

Skeletons in the Closet
THE FOLEY HOUSE INN
INVESTIGATION

Although the Foley House Inn is one of the busiest B&B's in town, they usually have at least one vacancy. *Photo by Ryan Dunn*

Just off of the north end of Chippewa Square sits the Foley House Inn. The square itself is one of the most famous squares in all of Savannah, due in large part to the blockbuster film *Forrest Gump*. All of the bus stop bench scenes were filmed at the north end of the square, and visitors to our great city seek out the spot where Forrest began his epic tale. The bench, unfortunately, is no longer there. It was placed there just for the film and then later removed, but a replica of the bench can still be viewed at the Visitor's Center Museum, located on Martin Luther King Blvd.

Chippewa square is also home to the historic Savannah Theatre, which is just one of many haunted locations that we have investigated. The Foley House Inn has quite a dark past, and it is definitely one of the most haunted inns in town.

THE HISTORY

The Foley House Inn is actually comprised of two large row houses that sit adjacent to each other. Although the Inn's sign is in front of 14 West Hull Street, the home located at 16 West Hull Street is also part of the inn. This structure was built in the year 1868 for a man named Dr. Lewis Knoor, who lived in the home until he died there years later, in 1896. Although we found a few other natural deaths in the home throughout the years, as it changed hands, the darkest history surrounding the Foley House Inn centers around the other half of the building located at 14 West Hull Street.

There was a prior structure that existed at 14 West Hull Street that was originally built for James and Mary Blois and their daughter, Lucille, in the year 1820. After James and Mary passed away many years later, Lucille Blois lived in the home until 1889, when the home was tragically destroyed by fire. There were three great fires in 1889 that ravaged the city of Savannah, and one of these fires burned down the First Presbyterian Church on Bull Street, as well as the Blois home at 14 West Hull Street. Seven years later, in 1896, the structure that currently sits at 14 West Hull Street was built. This home was built for a young widow named Honora Foley, who lived in the home with her widowed son-in-law, Captain James McIntyre, and her five grandchildren. A few years later, she died of heart failure, in 1914, in her upstairs bedroom.

AN APPARITION AND SKELETON

There are many ghost stories surrounding Honora Foley, and guests and employees have reported seeing her apparition throughout the home. As a widow, Honora Foley would take in boarders from time to time to make extra money. As the story goes, she awoke late one evening in her bed and saw a man standing over her watching her sleep. This was a gentleman to whom she had rented a room earlier that evening. Horrified beyond belief, she panicked and grabbed a candlestick holder off of the nearby night stand. She quickly bashed the man over the head with it, and he fell to the floor. After this, however, there is no other report of what later happened to this mysterious man.

In the mid 1930s, the structure was converted into Chippewa Apartments, and then it later became a private residence again. I did find records of a few natural deaths in the home over the years, but nothing that might indicate why it might be one of the most haunted inns in town. The building later became Beddingfield and Brown Physicians Office for a number of years, beginning in the early 1960s, and then it became the Foley House Inn Bed and Breakfast in 1983, which it remains to this very day.

Shortly after they opened, the inn was filling up quite regularly and they were in need of extra rooms. In 1985, only two years after purchasing the inn, the owners also purchased the adjacent row house at 16 West Hull Street. Two years later, in 1987, they decided to knock out a wall between the two houses to join them together on the inside by means of a small hallway. Since they were row houses and the homes sit right next to each other, this should have been an easy task. When they knocked out the wall, however, they made a shocking discovery. As the bricks tumbled down, a human skeleton fell out of the wall. Judging from the full decomposition of the corpse, it appeared that the body had been sealed in the wall since the early 1900s, and it was a male skeleton. The employees nicknamed him "Wally," for lack of a better name, as

The Foley House Inn, built in 1896 for a young widow named Honora Foley.
Photo by Ryan Reese

a dark joke, since the man was found in a wall. Could this have been the corpse of the man who was standing over Honora Foley's bed so many years ago? Honora Foley would have lived in the home during the years this body was sealed into the wall, so she must have known something about it.

The wall in which the skeleton was discovered was actually a secret room only a few feet wide. The room was built by a master mason judging from the brickwork, and the bricks themselves were made out of ballast stone. Ballast stone was used many years ago to balance out the cargo in the bottom of ships arriving from England and other European countries. They didn't need the stones on the return voyage home, so, in most cases, the stones were left in large rock piles along what is now River Street. Instead of leaving a large mess, Savannahians got very creative. They paved River Street with the ballast, as well as incorporated the stones into the construction and foundations of some early homes. (The structure that is now the Chart House on Bay Street is constructed primarily out of ballast.) Ballast stone was also nicknamed "ship brick" because of its use in balancing out these ships for so many years.

I spent over two years attempting to investigate the Foley House Inn, but I was always met with polite refusals. It wasn't until July of 2012 that I finally had the chance to set up an investigation. I was once again contacted by Frank Sulkowski of WJCL *ABC News* and WTGS *FOX News 28* about filming a third series of our television show, *Spooky Town*. I decided to try to contact the Foley House Inn once again to see if they would be interested in being a part of the show. This time, Grant Rogers, the inn's owner, readily agreed. As I do with all of our investigations, I set a date to come by and speak with him about the inn's history and activity.

As I sat in the parlor of the inn with Grant pouring over the many haunted stories involved with the place, I was in awe at the regal splendor that surrounded me. Although there was an underlying presence that could be felt there, the Foley House Inn was one of the most beautiful bed and breakfasts that I'd ever seen.

THE HAUNTS

According to Grant, there had been reports of hauntings ever since he purchased the place. One of the most frequent reports was that of the apparition of a male ghost who has been seen slowly pacing back and forth throughout the courtyard. This man is described as being in period dress with a top hat and cane, and he has frightened guests on more than one occasion. In addition, there have been numerous eyewitness accounts of a small girl with a large bow in her hair appearing in both of the inn's parlors. Almost as soon as she is seen, she is known to suddenly vanish into thin air. The most disturbing reports, however, concern a tall, dark shadow person that passes through the parlor and then disappears into the wall beside the fireplace.

THE INVESTIGATION

This investigation would be a proud notch in our belt, but it was even more exciting because this was the first official investigation of our two newest team members-Guieneverre Cutlip and Ryan Reese. Guieneverre joined us as our Marketing Director and Ryan Reese as our professional photographer.

We all arrived a few minutes after midnight and met the camera man, Biff Flowers, in the Inn's parlor. Biff informed us that Frank had just finished filming the late news and that he was on his way. As soon as we started to unpack, I turned on my audio recorder. Not five minutes had passed by before we caught our first piece of audio evidence in the front entranceway. A male spirit clearly whispered: "Who did it?" into my audio recorder. After later reviewing the evidence, I think the entity may have been asking about the body that had been sealed into the wall for so many years.

Throughout the evening, we were accompanied by Tyler Duddy, the Inn's concierge, who proved to be a great asset throughout the investigation. As we began walking through the home and documenting initial readings in humidity, EMF fields, and temperature, it wasn't long before we captured our second EVP, but this time it happened on the fourth floor of the 14 West Hull Street side of the home. In the hallway on the fourth floor, the voice of a male spirit growled: "You lied" into an audio recorder. Although this wasn't heard until the playback, this particular one still makes my skin crawl to this day. We were experiencing all kinds of paranormal activity within the first hour of being inside the building, but this was just the beginning.

ROOM 401

Guieneverre, who is a natural sensitive to the paranormal, had a strange personal encounter in room 401. As she was conducting an EVP session with Kim, our EVP Specialist, something stroked her left arm. She was sitting on the floor in the middle of the room, so there was nothing nearby that could have caused such a sensation. Later in the evening, Guien had a similar experience in room 402 when something tugged at the back of her shirt as she was seated on the floor. Yet again there wasn't a way to rationalize what had just happened.

MORE EVIDENCE

Throughout the evening, odd occurrences happened to everyone present. At around 1:45 in the morning, all investigators and the film crew began to smell a strong odor of something burning. It smelled as if there was a large fire in the room with them, yet there was not even a spark or sign of smoke to be found. Considering the fact that there was a fire that occurred there in 1896, and we could find no explanation for the odd occurrence, this may have been an unexplainable residual olfactory experience felt by all.

As the evening progressed we began to capture more and more audio evidence. Right outside Honora Foley's bedroom, an audio recorder captured two very loud, bloodcurdling, female screams that appeared to have come from inside the room. The screams were so loud that they should have been heard on location had they not been paranormal. I should have heard it with my own ears, since I was holding the audio recorder in my hand right outside the door at the time.

Some of the most compelling audio evidence captured at the Foley House, however, was caught right near the wall where the body was discovered in 1987. The secret room that used to conceal the corpse is now a small hallway with a mini staircase of about three to four stairs that joins the two halves of the inn together. Photographer Ryan Reese and I were seated on these stairs when we captured a chilling EVP of a male entity. As we were discussing the history of the home, a male voice whispered very loudly into my audio recorder, "I need another ship brick." Could this be the mason who bricked the body into the wall so long ago? The fact that this entity was asking for the same type of brick that the body was sealed into the wall with was very disturbing. Perhaps this spirit wanted to brick Ryan Reese and me into the wall, too.

Nonetheless, the paranormal activity in the Foley House kept increasing the longer we were there. About an hour later, as Kim and I were conducting another EVP session together in room 401, we caught one of the most disturbing EVPs of the night. We were asking about the body that was hidden in the wall for so many years, when a male entity growled "Who told?" angrily into my digital audio recorder. This voice was so clear and indignant, the clip sent chills down my spine.

We managed to capture twenty-eight EVPs altogether during our investigation of the Foley House Inn, many of which directly tied into the history of the home.

This location is also one of the first stops on our ghost tour, and I always enjoy having people on the tour who happen to be staying there. To this day, I regularly receive accounts of the paranormal, on an almost weekly basis, from guests staying at the Foley House Inn. This still remains to be one of the most haunted bed and breakfasts in Savannah. With all of the activity surrounding this old home, you should have a fair chance of coming into contact with the other side here. If you do choose to stay at the Foley House Inn, which I highly recommend, ask for Tyler, the concierge. He will make sure that you are more than taken care of during your stay in our beautiful city.

CHAPTER 16

HAUNTINGS IN THE HOME

A FEW PRIVATE-RESIDENCE CASES

Every year I receive hundreds of calls and e-mails concerning hauntings in the home. My paranormal investigation team, the Savannah Ghost Research Society, investigates these claims, although there have even been occasions where we have had to refer cases to other local groups due to our workload. Past Life Investigations of Georgia has been a great team that we continue to network with on a regular basis.

Private residential cases usually tend to be the worst calls that we deal with. Although the world of the supernatural is becoming more and more popular lately, many still disbelieve in the actual existence of ghosts. If you could imagine, however, being a skeptic, and then moving into an extremely haunted home—it isn't long before you are giving us a call. Throughout this book, I have used real names and locations in every story, up until now. Due to the sensitive nature of this material, and to protect the privacy of our clients, full names have not been used in most of the stories in this chapter.

INCIDENT ONE

In the fall of 2010, I received a call from a lady, who was experiencing intense paranormal activity in her home in North Georgia. She would wake almost every morning to find strange scratches all over her body. When she was in the bathroom getting ready for work in the mornings, she would see rotted dead hands reaching for her from behind as she stared into the mirror. Frightened and terrorized, she would turn around and look behind her, only to see nothing there. This, however, was only the beginning.

One evening, as she spent time with her boyfriend, things began to take a turn for the worse. As they were cuddled together on the couch watching a movie on television, VCR tapes began to lift up off the shelves and hurtle themselves through the air at the couple. The frightened pair scrambled towards the front door as fast as they could, and the videotapes continued to fly through the air at an alarming rate. Over the next few days, the activity in the home began to escalate. Strange noises could be heard coming from the attic at night as the couple lay in bed trying to sleep. It sounded as if furniture was being moved across the floor upstairs, and demonic growls could be heard as well. Unexplained foul odors began to permeate the air of the home, and more and more scratches began to appear both of their bodies after they would wake in the morning. Also, crosses that had previously been hung on the wall for protection were found to be unexplainably inverted on many occasions.

This was an extremely rare occasion in which the activity experienced may have quite possibly been of demonic nature. Although we specialize in even the worst ghost and haunting cases, we do not deal with demonic cases. We did, however, refer her to someone who handles such situations. In the paranormal community, there are those who study and deal with demonic cases. These people are known as demonologists. They are able to understand the hierarchy of these demonic entities and the inner workings of their plot against mankind. We were able to contact a demonologist who was able to aid this poor woman in her dire situation.

From the beginning of the case, this woman's boyfriend was adamant about our team not being involved in the situation. Every time she contacted us, she had to do it behind closed doors for fear of her boyfriend discovering that she was speaking to us. According to the demonologist that took over her case, the boyfriend was already possessed, and his reluctance of our being involved was actually the demonic entity itself trying to prevent anyone from banishing it from her home.

After multiple exorcisms of the house itself, which unfortunately led to a breakup between the couple, the woman is now doing fine. She has since had no more demonic encounters, but the horrors of what happened to her will haunt her memory for the rest of her life. After her close encounter with these demonic entities, she has now also become more involved with the Christian church.

INCIDENT TWO

One of the worst calls that I have ever received since becoming a paranormal investigator took place in 2011. We had been conducting paranormal investigations for a little over a year, and we were starting to get a lot of calls concerning disturbances in private homes. One early summer morning, the phone rang at about 9 a.m. The woman on the other end sounded very distraught. I tried to calm her down as best I could, and, after a few minutes, she began to tell me about her recent horrifying encounter with something that was possibly demonic. She went on to tell me that, although she was a married woman, she had been having an affair with a man named Tom for over a year.

One late Saturday night, she was talking with Tom on the phone while sitting in her living room. It was around three in the morning, and her husband and two children were fast asleep just down the hall. Not long into their conversation, Tom suddenly quit talking. The woman assumed that he had fallen asleep, considering the hour, yet she still had a strange feeling that something wasn't quite right. She couldn't go to check on Tom until Monday morning, because she wanted to wait until her husband was at work and her kids were in school, in order to prevent arousing suspicion.

She arrived at Tom's house that Monday morning at around 10 a.m. She pounded on the door for a few minutes, but Tom didn't answer. She did have a key to his place, since their affair had been going on for quite some time, so she decided to enter the home and check on him. She unlocked the door and walked into the house and, a moment later, she uttered a bloodcurdling scream. Lying on the living-room floor was Tom, motionless and void of color. According to the coroner's report, Tom had suffered a heart attack that past Saturday night, at approximately the same time he had stopped speaking to her on the phone that evening. In his dead hand he still held his cell phone.

The woman quickly grabbed the phone out of Tom's hand and started going through the recent call log. She wanted some kind of closure, and to know if she was the last person to speak to Tom before his untimely death. After quick review, it turned out that she was the last person to ever speak to him, but about twenty minutes after their conversation abruptly ended, there was a strange voicemail that appeared on his phone. The call showed up on the cell phone as coming from an unknown caller. After reviewing Tom's cell phone records later that month, it appeared that Verizon (the cell provider) had no record of this call—which was virtually impossible. The voicemail itself, however, is probably one of the most disturbing EVPs that I have ever heard.

A demonic voice can clearly be heard growling "I have Tom" on the voicemail. This is why the woman was so distraught when she called us. She knew that there wasn't anything anyone could do to help Tom, but she wanted some closure and to have someone verify that what she was experiencing was real. Due to the fact that Verizon had no record of the phone call, and the nature of the EVP itself, we were able to determine that this was a legitimate piece of paranormal evidence. Although there was no way to save Tom, we were able to offer her some closure as to the voicemail. She had known when she contacted us that there was no saving Tom; she just wanted someone to determine if the recording was real or not. Even two years later, this recording still manages to keep me up at nights and haunt my memory.

INCIDENT THREE

One of the most recent cases that we have handled concerned a family experiencing activity in their home in Port Wentworth, located right outside of Savannah. Their four-year-old daughter kept seeing the ghostly apparition of a small female child named Aubrey who would speak to her. Aubrey would tell this little girl to go and play in the streets, so that she could be with her forever. One night, very late into the evening, Aubrey apparently woke the child up and told her to go into the kitchen drawer and grab a sharp knife. She then told the child to slice her parent's throats open while they slept. Frightened by Aubrey's wicked scheme, the child raced back down the hallway to her room and buried herself under the covers. The following morning, she told her mother about the previous night's encounter. Concerned about the welfare of her daughter, the mother began to inquire more about this supposed ghost named Aubrey.

As the child's story began to unfold, the mother became more and more frightened for her daughter. Aubrey had told this little girl that she had been murdered in the home years before by her father, who then supposedly hung himself from one of the rafters. The child also told her mom that the reason she liked to play outside so much lately was because Aubrey couldn't come outside, her spirit was trapped inside the house.

The following evening, the paranormal occurrences in the home began to escalate. It was around four in the morning when the parents were suddenly awakened by the sound of their small child screaming at the top of her lungs from her bedroom down the hall. As the parents rushed into the room to check on their daughter, they were shocked at what they saw. The little girl was pinned to her bed by a dresser. Earlier that evening at bedtime, the dresser had been on the other end of the room. There is no possible way that this small four-year-old child could have moved that heavy dresser full of clothes all the way across the floor by herself. They rushed their daughter to the emergency room, where she was immediately treated for injuries and then sent home. The following week, I was contacted by the family to conduct an investigation at the home.

As with at least seventy percent of all the private residence cases that we take on, the family moved out before we could come out to investigate. In most of these types of cases, they wait until it's too late to call for help. By the time they contact our team, they have usually had about all that they can take. Even when we book an emergency investigation for the following night, we often get calls on the morning of the investigation date saying that they had to cancel, because they could not stay even one more night in the home.

The family is now living in a home outside Savannah's famed Historic District, and the child hasn't seen the ghost of Aubrey since they left the house.

INCIDENT FOUR

The most disturbing case that we have ever investigated, concerning a malevolent private residence haunting, occurred in September of 2012. We received an email from a young woman named Nicole Bork who was experiencing dangerous paranormal activity in her home. She lived on Hunter Army Airfield Base with her military husband and two-year-old son. Her husband had just returned from Afghanistan a few months before, and they had started experiencing paranormal activity as soon as they moved on base. The activity became so bad that her husband was temporarily hospitalized because of mental decline. Although one could easily argue that his hospitalization was due to Post Traumatic Stress Disorder (PTSD), the other family members' experiences couldn't be as easily explained.

Their two-year-old son was telling his mother that he would see a man standing outside his window every night watching him sleep. The mother would see a dark shadow person peek around the corner and watch her when she would lie on the couch at night and watch television. She would also wake in the middle of the night unable to breathe, with the sensation of some unseen force pressing heavily down on her chest. Her son's experiences became so intense that she had him taken out of the home to temporarily stay at his grandparent's house until the activity there subsided.

About a week later, Nicole left one afternoon to go grocery shopping. While she was at the store, her next-door neighbors witnessed a shadow figure staring back at them from the bay window in Nicole's home. The figure would disappear and then abruptly reappear again. When Nicole returned from the store a few hours later, her neighbors were waiting outside for her as she pulled into her driveway. As she got out of her car, they instructed her to stay outside while they searched the home. After examining the whole house, they determined that there had been no one in the home while Nicole was gone. They knew that they had clearly seen someone earlier, and they could not explain the apparition in the bay window. This dark shadow figure began to appear more and more over the following weeks, and the activity in the home continued to escalate even further.

Nicole eventually called us in to conduct an investigation to see what we could find. I arrived at the home that evening with just one other investigator, our marketing director Guieneverre Cutlip. We decided to keep a smaller group for this particular investigation, because this was a smaller home. This was to avoid any possible contamination of evidence caused by too many people on location. As soon as we set foot in the home, we could feel the presence of what Nicole had been dealing with. The air was very dense, and although the home itself was welcoming, the underlying presence of something much more sinister could be felt by all. We set up REM Pods, which are motion detectors that detect fluctuations and disturbances in energy. We set these pods up in the doorway where Nicole often saw the shadow person lurking. Within the first five minutes of being set up, they began to go off. We then began to capture some of the most unsettling pieces of audio evidence that we have ever caught.

One of the most disturbing EVPs we caught that evening was captured in Nicole's bedroom. We caught the recording of a malevolent male entity growling: "I'm gonna kill her tonight." Yet another EVP was captured in the home of a male entity whispering: "We will die." Due to all of the activity and the evidence captured there, Nicole no longer lives in the home. Although she lives in a new house, she still experiences paranormal activity on a daily basis. Nicole is one of the few people in this world who have the rare gift of being sensitive to the spirit world. The chances are, unfortunately, that wherever she goes, she will most likely continue to experience paranormal activity, from time to time, for the rest of her life. The good thing is, however, that the malevolent entities that plagued Nicole and her family no longer linger. She has started a new chapter in her life, but the incidents that occurred in her previous home will not easily be forgotten.

Many stories in this chapter have unexpected outcomes. The world of malevolent spirits and demonic entities is one not accepted by many, but it does indeed exist. Sometimes, even after multiple cleansings and exorcisms of a home, these entities still will not let up. In some instances, the people involved have to vacate their home and move to a new location to rid themselves of the activity. In other situations, they have been able to rid their home of these spirits, or figure out a way to coexist with them, if they aren't malevolent in nature. Nonetheless, there is never an easy answer in a case of a serious haunting. We always tell our clients that they can make it through this, but there is never a quick fix that works overnight. In many cases, multiple cleansings and exorcisms have been required to rid these homes of these negative spirits.

AFTERWORD

We still receive calls on an almost daily basis concerning paranormal activity in homes. In many cases, we are able to offer some assistance and understanding with these hauntings, but on occasion we do encounter an entity that will not rest until the family has vacated the home. Although these entities that haunt the place may have died years before, their spirit still lingers on, fighting to retain what was once theirs. Since these also tend to be the most personal cases, it is very easy to sympathize with the families and what they are going through. Dealing with torment on a daily basis from forces unseen is never an easy pill to swallow. Not only do these hauntings attack you physically, but they can get into your mind as well. Dealing with a haunting for any extended period of time begins to weigh on anyone involved, and we make our best efforts to provide comfort for those in any such situations.

My paranormal research team, the Savannah Ghost Research Society, continues to investigate paranormal claims throughout Savannah and the surrounding areas on a regular basis. Should you be in need of our services, please do not hesitate to contact us at (912) 665-8886. The evidence that we have captured over the years on our investigations is featured on our walking ghost tour company, Afterlife Tours. To book a tour with us, call (912)398-7820 or visit us at www.afterlifetours.net to make a reservation.

We are always here
and we are always available.

VISITOR AND CONTACT INFORMATION FOR HAUNTED LOCATIONS

In order to provide the opportunity for you to visit locations listed in this book, I have included contact and visitor information. (I have, however, omitted the private residence locations to protect the privacy of those involved.)

The Amethyst Inn
402 East Gaston Street
Savannah, GA 31401
(912) 234-7717
www.amethystinnsavannah.com

The Boar's Head Grill & Tavern
1 North Lincoln Street
Savannah, GA 31401
(912) 651-9660
www.boarsheadgrillandtavern.com

Hours of Operation:
Monday to Thursday 11 a.m. to 3 p.m.
and 5 p.m. to 10 p.m.
Friday and Saturday 11 a.m. to 3 p.m.
and 5 p.m. to 11 p.m.
Sunday 12 p.m. to 3 p.m.
and 5 p.m. to 9 p.m.

Bradley's Lock & Key
24 East State Street
Savannah, GA 31401
(912) 232-2148

Hours of Operation:
Monday to Friday 8 a.m. to 4:45 p.m.
Saturday 8 a.m. to 3 p.m.
Sunday Closed

The Chart House Restaurant
202 West Bay Street
Savannah, GA 31401
(912) 234-6686
www.chart-house.com/locations/savannah

Hours of Operation:
Lunch Saturday and Sunday
11 a.m. to 3 p.m.
Dinner Monday to Thursday
4:30 p.m. to 10 p.m.;
Friday 5 p.m. to 10:30 p.m.;
Saturday 3 p.m. to 10:30 p.m.;
Sunday 3 p.m. to 10 p.m.
Happy Hour 4:30 to 7:00
Monday to Friday

Colonial Park Cemetery
201 East Oglethorpe Avenue
Savannah, GA 31401

Cemetery Hours:
8 a.m. to 8 p.m. seven days a week

The Foley House Inn
14 & 16 West Hull Street
Savannah, GA 31401
(912) 232-6622
www.foleyinn.com

Fort McAllister Historic State Park
3894 Fort McAllister Rd.
Richmond Hill, GA 31324
(912) 727-2339
www.gastateparks.org/info/ftmcallister

Hours of Operation:
Monday to Saturday 8 a.m. to 5 p.m.

The Moon River Brewing Company
21 West Bay Street
Savannah, GA 31401
(912) 447-0943
www.moonriverbrewing.com

Hours of Operation:
Sunday to Thursday 11 a.m. to 11 p.m.
Friday and Saturday 11 a.m. to Midnight
Happy Hour 4 p.m. to 7 p.m. daily

The River Street Inn
124 East Bay Street
Savannah, GA 31401
(912) 234-6400
www.riverstreetinn.com

The Savannah Theatre
222 Bull Street
Savannah, GA 31401
(912) 233-7764
www.savannahtheatre.com

**Savannah Harley Davidson
on River Street**
503 East River Street
Savannah, GA 31401
(912) 231-8000
www.savannahhd.com

Hours of Operation:
Monday to Saturday 10 a.m. to 6 p.m.
Sunday 12 p.m. to 6 p.m.

The 17hundred90 Inn
307 East President Street
Savannah, GA 31401
(912) 236-7122
www.17hundred90.com

The 12 West Oglethorpe House
12 West Oglethorpe Avenue
Savannah, GA 31401

Warren A. Candler Hospital
516 Drayton Street
Savannah, GA 31401

BIBLIOGRAPHY

Auerbach, Loyd. *ESP, Hauntings and Poltergeists.* (New York, New York: Warner Books, 1986).

Bilbo, James. "Recent Lynchings of New York Men in Savannah; Narrative of the Sufferers." *The New York Times.* (1860, November 29).

Bondeson, Jan. *Buried Alive: The Terrifying History of Our Most Primal Fear.* (New York, New York: W. W. Norton & Co Ltd., 2002).

Cannell, J.C. *The Secrets of Houdini.* (New York, New York: Bell Publishing Co., 1989).

Caskey, James. *Haunted Savannah: America's Most Spectral City.* (Savannah, GA: Subtext Publishing, 2013).

Debolt, Margaret Wayt. *Savannah Spectres and other Strange Tales.* (Atglen, PA: Schiffer Publishing Ltd., 1983).

Durham, Roger S. *Guardian of Savannah: Fort McAllister, Georgia, in the Civil War and Beyond.* (University of South Carolina Press, 2008).

Estep, Sarah. *Voices of Eternity.* (New York, New York: Fawcett Publishing, 1988).

Gay, Evelyn Ward. (1983). *The Medical Profession in Georgia, 1733-1983.* (Atlanta, Georgia: Auxiliary to the Medical Association of Georgia, 1983).

Guiley, Rosemary Ellen. *The Encyclopedia of Ghosts and Spirits.* (New York, New York: Checkmark Books, 1992).

Historical Marker Database. www. hmdb.org. Jewish Colonists Marker. http://www.hmdb.org/marker. asp?marker=26707.

Historical Marker Database.- www. hmdb.org. Original 1733 Burial Plot Marker. http://www.hmdb.org/marker. asp?marker=9388.

Historical Marker Database. www.hmdb. org. Spring Hill Redoubt Marker. http://www.hmdb.org/marker. asp?marker=5475.

Historical Marker Database. www.hmdb. org. The Battle of Savannah Marker. http://www.hmdb.org/marker. asp?marker=18214.

Historical Marker Database. www.hmdb. org. The Great Yellow Fever Epidemic of 1820 Marker. http://www.hmdb. org/marker.asp?marker=5330.

Historical Marker Database. www.hmdb. org. Warren A. Candler Hospital Marker. http://www.hmdb.org/marker. asp?marker=15928.

Holzer, Hans. *GHOSTS: True Encounters with the World Beyond.* (Chicago: Black Dog and Leventhal Publishers, 1988).

Hough, Franklin Benjamin. *The Siege of Savannah (Papers of George Washington: Revolutionary War).* (Applewood Books U.S., 2009).

Hustmyre, Chuck. *Haunted Crime Scenes: The Murder of Samuel T. Baker*. www.trutv.com Crime Library. http://www.trutv.com/library/crime/notorious_murders/classics/samuel_baker/1_index.html.

Jones, Charles C. *The Siege of Savannah In December, 1864, & the Confederate Operations in Georgia & the Third Military District of South Carolina During General Sherman's March from Atlanta to the Sea*. (Albany, N.Y.: J. Munsell, 1874).

Levy, B. H. *Savannah's Old Jewish Community Cemeteries*. (Macon, Georgia: Mercer University Press, 1983).

Marcus, Jacob Radar. *The Colonial American Jew, 1492-1776*. (Detroit, Michigan : Wayne State University Press, 1970).

Morris, Bob. "Man in Black: Police Patience and Teamwork Ended Drifter's killing Spree." *The Savannah Morning News*. 1999, September 13.

Plechocinski, Elizabeth Carpenter. *The Old Burying Ground: Colonial Park Cemetery: Savannah Georgia 1750-1853*. (Savannah, Georgia: Oglethorpe Press, 1999).

Ryan, Jennifer Guthrie and Hugh Stiles Golson. *Andrew Low and the Sign of the Buck: Trade, Triumph, Tragedy at the House of Low*. (Savannah, GA: Frederic C. Bell Publisher, Inc.).

Schmitt, Ben. Serial killer faces charges in Savannah. *The Savannah Morning News*. 1998, March 26.

Usinger, Robert L. *Yellow Fever from the Viewpoint of Savannah*. United States Public Health Service.

Wakefield, Vivian. Florida Supreme Court Overturns Death Sentence of Killer. *The Savannah Morning News*. 1998, August 28.

Warren, Ed and Lorraine with Robert David Chase. *Ghost Hunters*. (New York, New York: St. Martin's Paperbacks, 1989).

Wilton, David. *Word Myths: Debunking Linguistic Urban Legends*. (Oxford University Press, 2009).

Word, Ron (July 5, 2003). *Gary Ray Bowles vs. State of Florida*. The Supreme Court of Florida, Case Number SC96732. October 11, 2001.

Zaffis, John and Brian McIntyre. *Shadows of the Dark*. (New York, New York: iUniverse, Inc., 2004).

"TO UNDERSTAND THE LIVING,
YOU'VE GOT TO COMMUNE WITH THE DEAD."
—MINERVA

FROM: *MIDNIGHT IN THE GARDEN OF GOOD AND EVIL*